The Deepest Valley

A DEVOTIONAL JOURNEY THROUGH CANCER, FEAR, DOUBT, AND HOPE

Dan Kallesen

ISBN (paperback) 978-0-578-74111-6

First Printing, 2020

THE DEEPEST
VALLEY

Contents

Dedication

I dedicate this book to **God**, whose love and strength are always with me. It is by His grace that I am able to travel this journey. All the glory goes to Him.

To my **mom and dad**, for their love and guidance over the years and the foundation they gave me.

To my **friends and family**, for their love, prayers, and support.

To my **doctors and nurses** for being great resources of God.

And to **you**, for taking this journey with me. I have been blessed by many, and I pray that in some way this book will be a blessing to you!

Preface

I am neither a trained theologian nor a professional pastor. I'm just a man of faith sharing a story of the mental, spiritual, and emotional battle I have gone through since my cancer diagnosis. However, I have been blessed by the fellowship and worship at Cross Church in Springdale, Arkansas. The pastors—Ronnie Floyd, Nick Floyd, and Jeff Crawford—have given me strength through their preaching of the Word and their weekly messages that have guided me through this difficult but impacting time. I am who I am today because of those deep valleys.

My theological and biblical commentary may not always be technically precise, but I hope this book will serve as encouragement as you walk through your own deepest valley.

Take the journey with me.

Dan Kallesen

The number one cause of stress is trying to be in control of what is out of your control. You are not in charge of what the world delivers to your doorstep. You are in charge of your response. Respond don't react!

Noah benShea

My Spiritual War with Cancer

It was in giving my older daughter a birthday present that I first saw the valley ahead of me. I had no idea how deep it was going to be, but it brought new meaning to that old saying, "Before you can receive, you must first give."

Summer was just around the corner and the only thing my daughter, Dani, wanted for her birthday was for me to call a doctor and schedule an appointment for a physical. She'd lost her mother that same year to colon cancer, and she needed the comfort of knowing her dad was in good health. She didn't want me to leave her, too.

It seemed like an easy gift to give her, but as I thought about it, I realized it had been a very long time since I'd had a physical exam. In fact, I didn't even have a doctor. Dani, however, was persistent during my procrastination.

How could I refuse?

I asked one of my best friends, a pharmaceutical rep named Martin, for a recommendation, and he sent me to Dr. Haws in Springdale.

I made the appointment and went in for what I fully expected would be a routine physical. The doctor did blood work and ran tests. Initially, everything seemed fine. We just had to wait for results from the blood work.

It was June, and baseball season was in full swing. My son Logan played on a travel team, and he had a tournament in Wichita that weekend. On Thursday afternoon I was getting packed and ready to leave when I received a call from the doctor's office. It was the nurse.

"Mr. Kallesen," she said. "You need to come into the office right away."

"I can't," I replied. "I'm leaving town."

"We'll make time for you," she said, "but you need to come in this afternoon."

I was ready to hit the road for Wichita. After the tournament, we planned to head to Lincoln, Nebraska, for a football camp. I wasn't supposed to be back in town until Tuesday.

Bear in mind, I had no premonition at this point that the nurse's call was a big deal. My father had died from heart disease, so I assumed they were going to tell me my cholesterol was high.

Finally, I agreed to postpone the trip a couple of hours and head to the doctor's office. When I arrived, I asked the nurse, "What's going on?"

"Mr. Kallesen, your PSA is really high," she replied.

I had no idea what PSA was. I'd never heard of it, but I began to sense that something was seriously wrong. Dr. Haws came into the room, and I could tell immediately he was in "very professional" mode (the kind of mode they adopt when they're about to deliver bad news).

"What's the problem, Doc?" I asked.

"Your PSA is the highest I've ever seen," he said. "I'm going to set you up with a urologist right away."

He went on to explain that PSA stands for prostate-specific antigen, which is a protein produced by the prostate gland. An elevated PSA is an indicator of cancer. While a normal PSA should be around 4.0 nanograms per milliliter of blood or less, mine was a whopping 1,400 ng/ml. To put that in perspective, a PSA of 10 ng/mL is considered dangerous.

It is difficult to express just how ill-prepared I was for this news. Life had been going very well for me and my family. I had gone through a difficult career transition after a layoff ten years earlier, but since then I had started my own business and sold it. Financially, we were on the upswing. My loving family had just moved into a beautiful new home. My son, Logan, and my younger daughter, Rylee, both were excelling as students at Shiloh Christian School. My oldest daughter was doing great in her career teaching fourth grade in Fremont, Nebraska. My relationship with my wife was as strong as it had ever been. Everything was great.

Suddenly, I'd been confronted with my own mortality, and I simply couldn't make the switch in my head. Out of the blue, I was in the fight of my life, and it was too much to accept! I immediately spiraled into despair and wanted to give up.

I made an appointment with a urologist for the following week, and then I went home in a fog.

My son had already left for the tournament with some of his friends, so I had to drive to Wichita by myself. I considered calling my wife—she was with our daughter, Rylee, at a volleyball tournament—but I couldn't bring myself to tell her about my appointment over the phone. Being a stereotypical male, I kept it all inside. I made the drive to Wichita without speaking to anyone, my mind racing the entire time. I completely lost track of the hours. Was my life over? I couldn't believe it. I prayed like crazy and listened to every Christian music station I could find on the radio.

When I arrived at the hotel in Wichita, my son and his team were enjoying a nice dinner. Everyone was laughing and having fun, but I just sat there, numb. After dinner, my son continued to hang out with his teammates, and I went up to my hotel room alone. I then made the unfortunate decision to search Google for information about prostate-specific antigen (PSA).

Google had nothing but terrible news for me. My worst fears were confirmed. I almost certainly had cancer, and the survival rate for someone at my age with my PSA was extremely low. I probably didn't have long to live. The prognosis was so bleak, I felt like I might roll over right then and die.

So many thoughts raced through my head.

How can this be? How am I going to tell my family? Why now? Why me? What did I do wrong?

Any small amount of hope I had was taken away by that Google search. My future was dark. I didn't have many days left.

I continued searching Google periodically throughout the weekend, looking for some good news. I found none. Still, I didn't tell anyone. I just tried to get it off my mind and enjoy the trip. When we arrived in Lincoln for football camp on Sunday, my daughter Dani came down to meet us. She lived nearby, so she joined us at the hotel.

Normally, I love watching football, and I love Nebraska, but my mind was racing the whole time. Even though I was surrounded by people, it was the longest, loneliest weekend of my life. That Sunday evening, we had dinner, and I still didn't say anything. I was struggling to come to terms with my impending death, and I couldn't bring myself to speak it out loud.

Football camp was on Monday, and we left right afterward, making the long drive home that evening. Still, no one in my family knew anything. I'd kept it all to myself and tried to bottle up the awful feelings.

I didn't tell my wife about my elevated PSA number until we arrived home on Monday night. Of course, I didn't share with her all of the awful things I'd read on Google, but I explained about my elevated PSA level and the upcoming urologist appointment. She could tell I was extremely worried, and she tried to comfort me as best she could.

"I'm sure everything will be all right," she said.

We cried, we prayed, and then we thought about poor Dani, who had just lost her mother to cancer.

How could this be? Why would God let this happen? It's not fair!

I had the urologist appointment and biopsy done that Thursday. The urologist was shocked at my PSA number. He later told me that my initial test results were so bad, my PSA so high, he had assumed there was something wrong with the test.

We'd already planned a family vacation to Destin, Florida for the following weekend, and Dani joined us on the trip. The biopsy results came back while we were there. The urologist confirmed my worst fears: I had prostate cancer.

Carla and I knew we had to break the news to the family, but we didn't want to ruin their vacation. We told the adult family members first: my brother-in-law and sister-in-law, my nieces and their families. Later, we found a private place, and I finally broke the news to Dani. We wanted her to have the time to let the news sink in before we got back home to Arkansas, because from there she would have the long drive to Nebraska by herself.

As you can imagine, it was an emotional conversation. I can't express how upsetting it was to see my wife and daughter in tears. Dani had been through so much with the loss of her mother, it broke my heart to add to her pain.

Still, even then, our faith made a difference. We felt a certain level of confidence, an undercurrent of hope, and now that my initial shock had worn off, I was able to tell them, "Listen, we're going to fight this. We will take it one day at a time, and we'll stay strong."

When we got home from Destin on Saturday, we broke the news to my other kids, Logan and Rylee. Dani stuck around to offer them support. We sat in the living room, and I told them about my diagnosis. That conversation was the most difficult one yet. In fact, it was one of the hardest things I've ever had to do in my life. Rylee was only twelve years old at the time, and Logan was sixteen.

As a family, we grieved. There were so many tears shed, so many hugs. I can still feel them today. The shock of the word "cancer" hitting a family is intense, but we turned to faith and prayer.

I met with the urologist again that week, and the news got even worse. His words during the appointment were ominous:

"Dan, this is very serious. We're not talking about normal prostate cancer. Do you understand? Your outlook isn't good. This is an aggressive cancer. You need to get your things in order."

Those words would come to haunt me.

Get my things in order?

He told me I had to select an oncologist. A friend of mine who had cancer recommended Dr. Rosenfeld at Highlands Oncology. Dr. Rosenfeld conducted scans that revealed that I was at stage IV. The cancer had spread; I had lesions on my spine and pelvis. He scheduled me for chemotherapy: six rounds of treatment, each of them set three weeks apart. The doctor made it crystal clear that my chemo treatments would be intense and side effects might be severe.

By this point, I was ready to start the fight of my life.

Dr. Rosenfeld encouraged me. "Look, someone has beaten every stage of cancer. It's not hopeless. We have a plan of attack."

God Had Prepared Me

Thankfully, though I didn't realize it fully yet; God had been preparing me for this battle for years. You see, ten years earlier, I had lost my cherished job. I'd worked at Sam's Club and Walmart for more than ten years, and I loved it there. However, during a round of layoffs, I was let go.

At the time, I thought it was the worst day of my life, but it proved to be one of my biggest blessings. As a direct result of losing my job, I wound up becoming an entrepreneur, meeting some great partners who trusted me, and starting a business with them. My family and I also started attending Cross Church in Springdale. But perhaps the best decision I made at that time was to start attending a men's group. That group would become an instrumental part of my support network during my battle with cancer.

More than that, losing the job I loved taught me how to put unhappy circumstances in God's hands and have faith in Him. There was a reason why I had been laid off. God had a purpose.

I went through some relationship struggles a few years ago, and while complaining to a friend about how I'd been wronged, he told me, "Hey, all you can do is fix yourself. You can't obsess over how you've been wronged." That advice would also prove instrumental during my battle with cancer. God had a purpose.

When my wife and I put our kids, Logan and Rylee, into Shiloh Christian School a few years ago, we had no idea how the school would rally around the kids after my diagnosis. Teachers and friends surrounded them with prayers and support. Rylee's classmates wrote a bunch of Scripture verses and words of encouragement on index cards and gave them to her. Her teachers would periodically pull her out of class to pray with her.

Two of Rylee's classmates just happened to be fighting cancer as well. The faith and strength of those two young men gave me hope. No one could have asked for better warriors of God to go to battle with.

Logan's football coach and teammates prayed with him. They had a team picture made with a banner that read, "Shiloh Football is Family...We are Praying for You." Each team member signed the picture.

God had a purpose in leading us to Shiloh Christian School. He was preparing our family for the coming battle, surrounding us with supportive people, even though we had no idea.

Treatment Begins

Before starting chemotherapy, you have to take a chemo class where they tell you what to expect, give advice for dealing with a compromised immune system, and provide meds to deal with possible side effects. The big bag of prescriptions from the pharmacy was intimidating.

Thankfully, when I started chemo, it wasn't as bad as feared—not in the beginning. I never had to use the big bag of side-effect meds. I truly believe the power of prayer helped keep the side effects at bay.

I started losing my hair after the first treatment, so I just shaved it all off. My son joined me in adopting the new look. Then a couple of players and their fathers from my son's baseball team also shaved their heads in solidarity.

By the time I completed the sixth and final round of chemo, I was feeling a lot weaker, but I was also elated. Chemo was done. I thought it was at the finish line, and I could finally get back to being my old self.

I couldn't have been more wrong. The cumulative effects of all that chemo attacking both the good and bad inside my body finally caught up to me after the final treatment. I was in more pain than I could have imagined. Every part of my body ached. My fingernails and toenails looked bruised, like someone had smashed them with a hammer. My whole body was utterly weak and broken.

Dr. Rosenfeld told me, "Look, there's a reason we stopped at six. This is all you can handle."

I realized I had not reached the finish line. On the contrary, I had a long way to go.

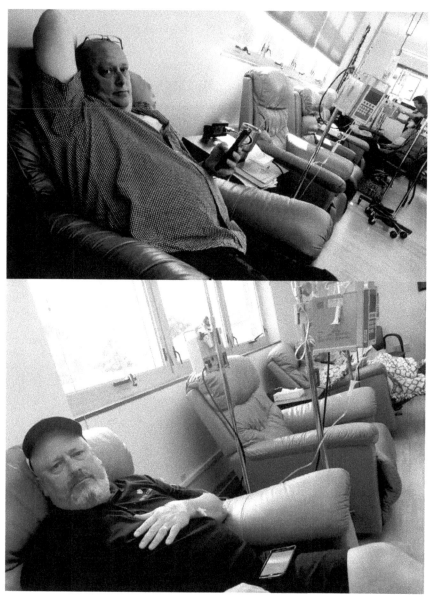

I spent a lot of time sitting in the chemo room, but it gave me
plenty of opportunities to pray and journal.

Breaking the news to my family was incredibly difficult, but it
brought us closer together. It's all about faith, family, and
friends!

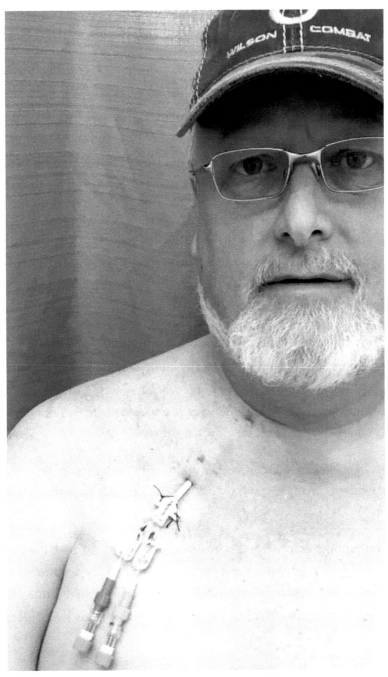

Getting ready for a series of three PROVENGE treatments to
fight the cancer that the chemo might have missed.

The Journal

I've always enjoyed reading devotional books. Shortly before I got laid off from Walmart, I had picked up a great book called *One Month to Live* by Kerry Shook, Senior Pastor of Woodlands Church in The Woodlands, Texas. I read through that book cover to cover, and it greatly impacted me.

In it, Kerry writes, "Why wait until you've been told you only have one month to live to truly live?" This question would come back to me many times during my battle with cancer. I loved the book and handed out hundreds of copies to my family and friends.

Another devotional book that made a big impact on me was *The One Year Uncommon Life Daily Challenge* by Tony Dungy. Seeing how Tony practiced his faith in his daily life helped me. It was so impactful that I read through it a second time with my son. As before, I handed out many copies to friends and family, a must read!

Books like these helped me start my days with Scripture, faith, and encouragement, laying a groundwork for the difficult days that were to come.

Several months before my cancer diagnosis, I needed a new book, so I went to the local bookstore and picked out a nice daily devotional with a leather cover. It was called *God's Wisdom for Today* by Johnny Hunt. I flipped through the first few pages and thought, "This looks nice. I'll give it a try."

What I didn't realize is that the book had a bunch of blank lines where readers were supposed to write their own journal entries. If I'd seen that, I never would have bought the book. English was my worst subject in school! Fortunately, I didn't find out until it was too late.

Reluctantly, I started journaling, but I soon realized the benefits of it. By the time I received my diagnosis, I'd been journaling for about eight or nine months. This would prove to be tremendously helpful.

When you're suddenly faced with your own mortality, you begin a life or death war within your own mind. In fact, I learned that the real battle is mental. Faith vs. fear, trust vs. doubt, acceptance vs. blame—it is intense, and it is constant. In the midst of my battle, I couldn't sleep very well, so I had to keep my mind occupied. I began writing about my internal battle, sharing my thoughts, struggles, and encouragements as I bolstered my faith. It was a way to remind myself continually that God is good.

At the same time, I'd written a few emails to my men's group asking for their prayers and updating them on my situation. I was surrounded by loving and supportive people, and I made the important choice not to hold back. So many of us guys refuse to open up to others, but in my emails, I admitted I was scared and needed help and prayers. Those emails merged with my journaling, as I began sharing my journal entries with the men's group.

Eventually, I began doing this weekly, and the circle of people reading my journal grew and grew. I'm still writing those journal entries to this day. In them, I offer Bible verses and quotes that have impacted me that week, thoughts and struggles I'm having, encouragements and prayers. Opening up to my friends and family in this way has completely transformed me. I'm a better man than I was before my cancer diagnosis, and I understand more than ever the importance of faith, family, and friends.

The War Within

When you're dealing with cancer, a catastrophic illness, or any other personal tragedy or hardship, the biggest part of the battle is the war within. Learning how to wage war in your mind against the negative thoughts and feelings that want to destroy your faith and hope is key to your survival. The journal entries I share in this book are a record of my own ongoing mental battle against the negative voices that wanted to stir up doubt, fear, blame, and self-pity.

This book is a record of how I dealt with my deepest valley. Daily, I had to *choose* to walk in faith. Through these last few years, my faith has become stronger, but I've also learned that the battle isn't really about cancer—and it's not really about me. This is about fighting the good fight of faith.

I haven't included all of my journal entries. Since 2016, I've written around 700,000 words! Therefore, these entries are merely a sampling, chosen specifically to give a sense of the internal struggle I went through (and continue to go through).

I share them with you now in the hope that they will encourage you wherever you are in your own journey. Maybe, like me, you're fighting cancer or some other disease. Maybe you're going through a personal tragedy or a time of deep discouragement. Everybody is fighting something!

You can use this book as a **daily devotional**, incorporating one entry a day into your regular quiet time, or you can read it at your own pace (though it is not really intended to be read all in one sitting). It is not, strictly speaking, a narrative, nor was it written with any specific structure in mind. In fact, you will obverse that the journal entries change over time, becoming more focused and purposeful. However, they provide an ongoing record of the battle one goes through when confronted with a life-changing hardship. Maybe some of the things the Lord taught me along the way will help you.

I have included blank spaces and extra pages so you can write your own thoughts and feelings after each entry. Remember, we are all in this together!

My Faith vs. Satan's Cancer

From this point on, I will share with you some of the entries I wrote during the last few years as I've journeyed through my deepest valley. I hope they will encourage you in your own journey. In some of these entries, I've included advice or questions to help you think about your own life, but I never intend to speak from a position of superiority. I am learning and growing every day—just like you!

Remember, we are stronger together.

"Carry each other's burdens, and in this way you will fulfill the law of Christ."(Galatians 6:1 NIV)

In Christ, our victory is assured.

Chemo: The First of Six Rounds

As I sit here taking in all of this chemo drip by drip, knowing the side effects it could have, it really makes me think. I know the journey the drugs are taking within me. Chemo attacks all of the bad cells along with the good ones as it travels through my body. How will it affect my body and mind?

In terms of my body's reaction, when I start feeling bad, I just take another drug. But then that drug also has possible side effects. It seems like this could go on and on.

In terms of my mind's reaction, I can only commit everything to my faith. A mind full of faith brings peace, and a mind at peace helps the body heal. I thank God for my family and my brothers and sisters in Christ.

There is no drip-by-drip in this spiritual treatment. Instead, I have received a tidal wave of prayers and support, both for me and for my family. All of these prayers attack the bad head on, take away the worry, and calm my fears, feeding the good with courage, strength, and wisdom.

As I look through the window and see the storm passing by today, it reminds me how blessed I am to have faith in our Lord and in all of the brothers and sisters who walk with me step by step on this journey.

Choosing to Trust Something Greater

The first week of treatment is done, and what a week. All of the prayers and support have been so humbling. I truly feel them and have been so blessed.

I had surgery on Thursday. They put a port in my left shoulder. All went well, but the lingering effects of the surgery made me feel like a zombie (I would make a good zombie). By the way, Carla said God gave me hair for a reason, so I don't think I'm going to be able to keep the new bald look.

It was supposed to be a week of waiting, but I'm not very good at waiting. I catch myself worrying; there is just so much information to take in. When that happens, I go to God in prayer. I realize this is going to be a test of endurance. I can choose not to worry about the side effects or the "what ifs."

There are so many reasons to be anxious about today and full of fear about tomorrow. The voices inside of me and the voices around me are not always on my side. Some of them create doubt, discouragement, speak harm to me, and deceive me. I know their game plan is to destroy me, both emotionally and spiritually. They want me to feel sorry for myself, to feel weak and anxious. They tell me, "You should be terrified about what is happening to you."

I choose not to be scared. Instead, I am thankful for being so blessed, and I choose to trust the One who is greater and wiser than me. His Word gives me wisdom, guidance, and strength for every situation in life. He has blessed me with my family, with skilled doctors, and with many brothers and sisters in Christ who offer their prayers and support at just the right time. They give me strength to fight off those voices of doubt and fear. Their prayers on my behalf keep away the side effects. Already, my PSA (prostate-specific antigen) numbers are dropping.

I know I have a long and hard fight ahead of me. I have five more treatments coming with many weeks in between each one. However, all of your prayers give my mind and body the strength and endurance they need.

My friend Noah gave me a note that I read often:

"Each of us is the source of the other, and our only strength is in knowing this."

I'm stronger with you, and I truly feel your prayers.

The Treasure of Family and Friends

The second week of treatment is done, and I have felt an overwhelming sense of the Lord's presence and power through His Word and through all the prayers coming from my brothers and sisters in Christ. The love of Jesus gives me the strength I need and provides for all my spiritual needs.

From my daily devotional, I want to share these wise words:

"I will lift up my eyes to the hills from whence comes my help. My help comes from the Lord, who made heaven and earth." (Psalm 121: 1-2 NKJV)

It is truly amazing how the Lord prepares us for our trials. I feel very blessed for all the prayers and support my family has been given. True treasures.

Last week I talked about the dark voices in me and around me that bring doubt, discouragement, and anxiety. The dark side is always trying, but this week the voices of angels were all around me. Those angels spoke through many of you in your text messages, emails, phone calls, and visits. I cannot thank you enough for the strength they bring.

This week at the men's group, I received unbelievable love, prayer, and support from a great group of brothers who are always there for me and for each other. I've always said one of the reasons women live longer than men is that they receive support from each other, and they are willing to rely on that support. I owe so much to my brothers, and I thank God for giving me the confidence to open up to them. It has brought such peace!

I have learned that one of the ways the Lord works is through the people he brings into our lives. That's why I tell my kids, "Choose your friends wisely. It's not all about the great times you will share. Your friends will also support you in your time of need."

I feel good this week. I'm keeping ahead of the side effects. I still can't believe cancer can be so stealthy. I only went to the doctor in the first place at the request of my daughter, Dani. Today is her birthday, and what a blessing she is. Thanks to her intuition, I was able to start fighting the cancer head on before the real ugliness showed itself.

The second three-week protocol of my cancer treatment will begin Monday morning. Again, thanks for your prayers. They give me the strength and endurance I need.

He is with us. He is in us. He is for us. For that, we are blessed!

Remembering My Football Days

It's week three of the three-week protocol, and I have completed two of six rounds of treatment. I am very thankful to get the second round behind me.

As we were sitting there on Monday morning for my three hours of drip-by-drip chemo, I told Carla, "At least all of these drips were outnumbered by all of the prayers coming our way." Boy, am I thankful for those prayers. The treatment is very aggressive, attacking both the bad and good in me. That's why the prayers and support are so important. I need the strength they give me—they rebuild the good that is in me.

In one of the books we discussed in our men's group, I read something that went like this: "When you operate according to reason, all you see is how deep the valley is. When you operate according to faith, you see how small the valley is compared to our all-powerful God."

God has blessed us with so much, I don't even know where to start. If I tried to mention everything, it would never end. I thank Him for every day. God is so hard at work in this journey. It humbles me. I have become more open to sharing my thoughts and experiences than I ever thought I could be. In fact, some of you who have known me for a while are probably shocked at how open I am now.

Remember, God didn't intend for us to be self-sufficient or independent. He doesn't want us to isolate ourselves in a time of need. One thing that hurts me is seeing other people going through the same fight without sharing their journey, without having the support of loving people who listen. Seeing people go through this struggle in isolation has brought me to tears.

I never realized how important it is to share with others in a time of need and uncertainty, and I thank God for surrounding me with family and friends as I go through this battle. Again, guys, the women have this figured out far better than us. They are far more willing to open up to their friends.

We are all stronger when we're together, which is why I have never been stronger than I am today. This has been a tremendous learning experience for me, but it has taken me many years to figure it out.

God has so many ways of teaching us, and in each lesson my faith in Him gets stronger and I become more confident for the next experience. He uses our experiences to show us our need for him, and He puts people in our lives to join us on the journey. It is a blessing to lean on them. He has also given us His Spirit.

"For God did not give us a spirit of timidity, but a spirit of power, of love and of self-discipline." (2 Timothy1:7)

Pardon me for using a football metaphor (maybe this is a time when the women can learn something from the men). In football, it takes a **head coach** to lead the team to victory. In life, we have a great head coach in the Holy Spirit.

In football, it takes a **united team** where everyone is committed to the same thing. The team is comprised of many different people—some big, some fast, some with a strong arm for throwing, others with a nose for the ball—all working together to overcome the opponent and win.

Every teammate has to work together to run a successful play: offense, defense, special teams, even the underclassmen.

In life, we are surrounded by a team of people from many different parts of our lives. If we're willing, we can share a common bond with them as we all travel through our individual adversities, working together to build each other up, strengthened by God's Word.

We need all types of friends, not just those who think exactly like us. We must be willing to invest in those friends. Avoid too much uniformity in your group. If everyone looks, talks, and thinks alike, your time may be unproductive, bad ideas may never get challenged, and you might not get a broad enough perspective to see what the Lord is up to.

In football, it takes a **game plan**, knowing your team's strengths and weaknesses, knowing your opponent's strengths and weaknesses, in every part of the game. In life, we must remember that we are sinners, that we are weak, and that our strength comes from the Lord and His Word. We must remember that Satan is a tough opponent who is attacking us from all sides, and we must be ready to resist his schemes.

In football, it takes **practice** and a coach constantly reminding us that we will play in the game just like we play on the practice field and in the off season. In life, we must be ready, keeping our faith strong, knowing that the game can change at any time, and surrounding ourselves with friends. We need a daily relationship with the Lord. We can't wait for the day of trouble to fall on our knees.

In football, we have **fans**—some good, some bad—from both sides of the field. We have the Monday morning quarterbacks. We have the fans who don't understand the game or the importance of teamwork. Some of them can be negative. Some can create distractions. We mustn't react to the negative. Instead, we must allow the good fans to inspire us as we move toward the goal together.

In life, it comes down to the people we choose to spend time with. It's tough to transform a negative group—it's more likely they will transform you. Find a group that will move with you toward the goal, encouraging and inspiring one another. Stay humble as you journey together and give all credit to the Lord.

Yes, it truly is amazing what you can learn from the game of football. I haven't played in many years, but I still remember the lessons I learned. My high school coach, Mr. Winkler, and my great teammates made an impact on me. In the four years I played, we only lost two regular-season games, and we won a state championship and made it to two other state playoffs.

Coach Winkler made us all better, and he helped us become great teammates. We were committed to doing whatever the team needed. We learned the difference between pain and injury, and we learned we can live with pain. All that Coach Winkler taught me is still with me today—and still relevant to my life. Coach had a "word of the week" for every week of the season. The word of the week for me right now is *endurance*. For my new season in life, I need to learn endurance.

Remember, everything is part of God's plan. Everything.

It's All About Attitude and Endurance

It's week four. Two chemo treatments out of six are behind me.

I received great news last week. The power of prayer is working! I feel good, and my new hairless look is fine, maybe a little scary; it's much easier to just shower and go now. I like it for that reason.

It's amazing how quickly your attitude can change if you allow it to. The secret to standing fast is *trusting* more than *trying*, *being* more than *doing*. I still remember what it was like receiving the bad news—feels like it was yesterday.

"You have cancer."

I can't begin to tell you the impact of those three words, but that is where my journey began. Since then a fire has been sparked in me by many friends (old and new), family, the men's group, my church, God's Word, and lots of reading.

The journey that follows those words—*you have cancer*—cannot be run alone. Fear takes root quickly, and you have so many questions. Those discouraging voices, both within and without, begin right away, and shock sets in.

"Why did this happen to me? What did I do to deserve this? Wait, I might die! How do I survive? According to Google searches, I should do this, do that, not do this, not do that. How can this be happening inside of me when I don't even feel sick? The sky is falling!"

You have to respond in faith:

"Hey, look up and breathe. Slow down. Remember that life isn't fair, and it isn't easy. You've experienced bad times before, and you've been fearful before, but your faith has always gotten you through. Trust God. He always has a plan. Allow Him to work through you. It is His will that shall be done. Our God is full of grace, and His love for us is great. He sees where we've been, He knows what's in our hearts, and He sees where we are going."

"Where there is no vision, the people perish." (Proverbs 29:18)

I will accept and trust His vision for my life. It all starts with my attitude. When you tie your attitude to your faith, it creates a powerful combination.

I know my God stands for love and life. I also know that the author of sin, the thief who comes to destroy and take what does not belong to him, is Satan. And what a great tool he has in cancer. Always remember, he is after us, and he has many tools. He plays by no rules, and he wants no credit—he just wants us to blame God.

Fortunately, I already know who has won and who will win in the end: our God. He is the one I want on my side. The Holy Spirit lives in me, and He urges me every day to live and love abundantly no matter the journey I'm on. I just have to take things one day at a time and trust.

How do I handle the fear? By expressing it, sharing it, talking with family, friends, and doctors, and turning it all over to the Lord. I express it as I write this. It is, after all, important to admit to the fear. I accept it. Fear is a reality in me, and I have to find healthy ways to let it out. The best way to do that is to share it with others. (Men, we can share our fears, too!)

What great support I have in all of you and in our Lord.

"In the day when I cried out, you answered me, and made me bold with strength in my soul." (Psalm 138: 3)

God is working through each of us.

"For everything that was written in the past was written to teach us, so that through endurance and encouragement of the Scriptures we might have hope." (Romans 15: 4)

I am humbled by all the prayers, texts, emails, calls, and visits. You give me strength and hope, which help me maintain the right attitude, building in me a deeper faith which I need for my physical, mental, emotional, and spiritual well-being as I wage war against this cancer.

Cancer won't destroy me. Together, we will send it, and its owner back where they belong, defeated, because we are stronger together in our faith.

"He who has begun a good work in you will complete it." (Philippians 1: 6)

I love and thank you all, as always. I know the source of the good news. When bad news hits—and it will—remember that it's all about your attitude.

Choose daily to look up.

Beware the Thief Who Plays by No Rules

It's week five, and two rounds of treatments out of six are behind me. I've had a great week. My energy level is high, and I haven't really had any headaches, unlike with my previous treatment.

Carla had been putting off a surgery that she needed, so we finally agreed that she should go ahead with it. There was never going to be a good time, so why continue to wait? She had the procedure done last week. All went well, but since the surgery was on her left thumb, she will only have one good hand for a while. Unfortunately, Carla having only one useable hand is more than my two hands can handle, so the family had to pull together and cover for Mom while she recovers. This is a family in need, and it hit us hard. We're panicking, unsure of what lies ahead.

With help from friends, we're getting by. Not only do I look like Mr. Clean these days, but I now know how he feels! Please pray for a quick recovery for Carla and the whole family. Carla's care has helped me feel better and have extra energy. She has been amazing, taking care of both the kids and me.

In a similar way, God cares for us with His love always and forever. We are so blessed to put our faith in a loving God, a loving family, and loving friends. Even with all of that, it doesn't mean life is going to be easy. We have to be wise, especially when we travel through the valleys of life.

"A wise person thinks much about death, while the fool thinks only about having a good time now." (Ecclesiastes 7:4 NLT)

Wisdom keeps us mindful that we have an enemy who exists for no reason other than to create doubt, confusion, fear, anxiety, and frustration. This thief wants to take what doesn't belong to him, and he is relentless in attempting to do so. He plays by no rules, and there are no boundaries. He will attack us wherever he can, and he uses everything at his disposal. Satan is trying to steal all of our dreams away, so we need to be mindful of his tactics. Faith is so important. I have never understood this more clearly than I do now.

"The thief's purpose is to steal and kill and destroy. My purpose is to give life in all its fullness." (John 10:10 TLB)

"Faith is to believe what you do not see; the reward of this faith is to see what you believe." (St. Augustine)

I'm blessed by all the prayers you are sending my way. I truly feel them, and I am stronger as a result. We can't let the thief steal anything from us!

In God's Strength, We Are Stronger

It's week six of treatment. I will start the third round of chemo soon.

This week I have been reminded of many things. I still feel all the prayers, and they are working; the prescriptions they gave me for the side effects remain unopened. Thank you, Lord. My energy level is high, so I've been able to visit people. We are all stronger together, and our strength comes from one another and from Him. It is clear to me now that we learn more from life's trials than from life's triumphs. We don't often learn the whys, but we do come to understand how much God loves us. All we have to do is surrender every area of our lives to Him.

I'm learning that as I walk with the Lord, surrounded by so many prayers, my vision is becoming clearer than ever. I see so much more. People have asked me why I feel so calm. They've asked Carla, "Does he really feel as good as he acts?" Yes, I do.

Satan throws fear at us daily. The key to overcoming it is to be overcome with the fear of the Lord. In my understanding, fear of the Lord means having a healthy respect for the majesty of God. Fear of the Lord strengthens my faith, drives out all other anxieties, and gives me peace of mind. If I fear the Lord, I do not need to fear anything else.

"He will fulfill the desire of those who fear him; He also will hear their cry and save them." (Psalm 145: 19 NIV)

He knew all there is to know about us before we even existed. He knows how many breaths we will take before our last. He knows our every thought before we think it. He hears our every word before we speak. He knows all of our motives. He sees every hurt and every weakness. The God who is three in one is the source of all wisdom. God is all-powerful, and I am utterly weak on my own. Only through faith in Him do I have strength. By faith, I have no need to fear anything.

"God is our refuge and strength, always ready to help in times of trouble. So we will not fear when earthquakes come and mountains crumble into the sea." (Psalm 46: 1-2 NLT)

Satan is alive in this world. We see this in the lack of love, in all of the sickness and pain, in the wars and fighting. We see it in our government, which has been trying to eliminate the very foundation of our lives, families, country, schools, and churches for years. Fear of the devil and fear of man will rob us of the best that God has in store for us. We must put our trust in the right place—in our all-powerful God who knows all!

I am stronger because of your prayers and my fear of our Lord. Spread the Word! Cancer is not the only fight we need to win.

Trust Is an Amazing Treasure

I had a doctor visit on September 8.

Trust is an amazing treasure. It does not come easy, and you can lose it quickly. As this journey continues, I am thankful for many things, but I am most thankful for my trust in the Lord. He is my solid foundation. Beyond that, I am thankful for all of the support and prayers that continually strengthen me and help me hold on to that trust as I walk through this deep valley.

"Trust in the Lord with all your heart and lean not on your own understanding; In all your ways acknowledge Him, and He shall direct your paths. Do not be wise in your own eyes; Fear the Lord and depart from evil. It will be health to your flesh, and strength to your bones." (Proverbs 3 :5-8)

This day started out great. In the morning, I had my men's group, and we read the following in our study: "Find ways to express your fears. Keeping your feelings to yourself has a debilitating effect on your immune system."

We talked about how I have been able to share my feelings through these journal entries. They allow me to release those fears, and that, in turn, helps my body heal. All of this is empowered by prayer.

When I was first diagnosed, my PSA (prostate-specific antigen) number was 1,400, the highest the doctor had ever seen. On July 7, my PSA dropped to 831. By August 15, it was down to 240. Today, September 9, we learned my PSA is only 49 as a direct result of the second round of chemo. Praise the Lord!

The doctor said this is a sure sign that the cancer is leaving my body.

I thank you again for all of your love, support, and most of all, your prayers.

God is good.

Starting the Day in God's Wisdom

It is week seven, and I have now completed three treatments. I am halfway done!

My PSA number is falling like a rock, and I feel good. My third round of chemo out of six is behind me, and I had no complications. Thank you, Lord. It is truly the power of prayer at work.

Still, it is sad seeing the effects of cancer and chemo on my body. It takes so much to heal. The doctors and nurses have such grace in caring for us. I thank the Lord for them. They are conduits for His healing process, and we are blessed that God uses all of His resources in our time of need.

As I reach the halfway point in my treatment, I have also reached the end of my daily devotional, God's Wisdom for Today. I began reading it a year ago, and I just reached the last day this week. I can't tell you how important it has been to start each day in God's Word. His wisdom is my strength for whatever may come.

A year ago, when I started the book, I never could have foreseen what was coming. Fortunately, I have not had to deal with it alone. None of us have to deal with our hardships alone. God is always there for us, and He provides us with many resources, if we're willing to use them.

You're not going to believe this, but the last page of my devotional shared words of wisdom from a high school football coach. I love this time of year: football season. I learned so much from my high school football coach. His wisdom has helped me throughout my life.

As I read the coach's words in my devotional, I remembered how many times I heard similar words from my own coach—and they still apply to everyday life. Two things in particular that he always emphasized:

1) Don't beat yourself.

2) Practice the fundamental disciplines of the game.

It really is that simple. That's wisdom, and wisdom keeps us from beating ourselves, thereby handing the game over to our opponent (or handing ourselves over to sin). Wisdom teaches us how to discipline our thoughts, words, and deeds to keep ourselves in check.

Coach, I'm ready. Put me in the game.

You never know when the enemy is going on the offense, so we have to be ready at all times. If you're not in the middle of a tough play, spend your time getting ready because it's coming. Surround yourself with great teammates, listen to your head coach, and be prepared.

When I heard the word "cancer," I knew I was suddenly in the fight of my life. The time for practice and preparing was over. Did I remember everything the Coach had told me? Did I remember all the wisdom He had shared with me? I was about to be put to the test.

I never wanted to be in this kind of game, but I've got the best play-caller of them all and I'm surrounded by great teammates. I've had a lot of practice, even though I would rather have skipped this game. However, we never know what the enemy is going to throw at us. We don't always get to choose the game. Sometimes, the stakes are as high as they can be.

That's why we should always be ready. Don't wait until the offense charges. Start listening to the Coach now, surround yourself with great teammates now, and remember the game plan. Be ready at any moment because the enemy doesn't wait for a convenient time.

For me, the fight is on!

Fortunately, I have great teammates helping me and the best possible Coach calling the plays. Together, we are pushing back against this cancer, and we are winning. It's all about playing hard to the end of the fourth quarter!

I can tell you this. As I head into the third and fourth quarters, I have never felt so confident or so loved. I almost feel sorry for the opponent. The thief is going home a loser!

Thank you for being on my team. Thank you for sending your prayers to the greatest play-caller of them all—our wise and loving God. We have a winning team. I am so blessed.

I end this week's entry by sharing one of the first prayers I ever wrote in my daily devotional. From September 2015:

"I pray for strength and wisdom in my words, thoughts, and deeds, so that I may be an example to others, showing them God's power through me and what God can do!"

I Surrender, I Trust, I Obey

It's my eighth week, and three treatments are done.

I continue to feel good, and I continue to be blessed by your prayers and support. You humble me every day.

The Lord is at work throughout my journey. He has placed people in my life to remind me that He is in control. One of those people gave me a great recommendation, and I want to share it with you.

He said, "When you first wake up in the morning, and again when you lay your head down at night, pray, 'I surrender, I trust, I obey.'"

It's a great suggestion that I will begin to implement every day.

Surrendering to His will has more to do with *being* than with *doing*. It is chiefly about our attitude toward God, toward others, and toward ourselves. *Righteousness* comes from a *right attitude*, and I am learning that it brings peace of mind to a body in need of healing.

What Is Faith?

It is week nine, and three treatments are done. I feel good, but my body keeps reminding me that faith and endurance are more important than ever. Sometimes, I'm a bit grumpy, but I know I am blessed.

Tomorrow I will begin the fourth chemo treatment of six. On Thursday I will meet with the doctor to find out my numbers from my most recent blood work. Please, keep the prayers coming. I have a big week ahead of me!

I have begun to think of my battle as "my faith vs. Satan's cancer."

But what is faith? Faith isn't believing that God can, it is knowing God will.

I understand now that my faith is constantly being tested. Sometimes my faith is strong, and other times it is weak. The kryptonite of my faith are those voices that keep whispering, "How can you feel this good when you have cancer and you're going through chemo? Something must not be working. The cancer must be spreading. The chemo probably isn't working."

The voices whisper these negative things to me daily. They tell me that I deserve this cancer because of my sins. They tell me I am not worthy of God's love. They tell me I should blame God, that I should be mad at God.

Life isn't fair. There is a dark side, and we all must deal with it sooner or later. We are in a battle with the evil one for our minds and our souls. We all have these negative voices inside of us, but we don't have to listen. We *mustn't* listen because these voices are the way Satan speaks to us.

Through faith, I know this:

"The fruit of the Spirit is love, joy, peace, patience, kindness, goodness, faithfulness, gentleness, and self-control." (Galatians 5: 22-23 NIV)

Through faith, I know this:

"Not only that, but we rejoice in our suffering, knowing that suffering produces endurance, and endurance produces character, character produces hope, hope does not put us to shame because God's love has been poured out into our hearts through the Holy Spirit who has been given to us." (Romans 5: 3-5 NIV)

Through faith, I know this:

"All things work together for the good to those who love God, to those who are the called according to His purpose." (Romans 8: 28)

Through faith, I know this:

I'm in the hands of the Great Physician, and He is using all of His resources to heal me: my mind, body, and spirit.

Through faith, I know this:

My sins are forgiven because He gave His only Son to die on the cross for my sins.

Through faith, I know this:

God is love.

Through faith, I know this:

"The fear of the Lord is the instruction of wisdom, and before honor is humility." (Proverbs 15:33 NIV)

Through faith, I know this:

I live for tomorrow, not today. I live for the love of Jesus, not for the things of this world. I live for heaven.

Through faith, I know this:

I am stronger with all of my brothers and sisters in Christ praying for me.

Through faith, I know this:

I must surrender. I must trust. I must obey.

From one of you I received the following message:

> It is easier to be *religious* than to be *righteous*. The pursuit of righteousness is a lifelong journey that is filled with discovery. To be righteous, we have to lean on our Lord and not on ourselves. God doesn't want our religion; He wants us.

We have *not* been promised that everything that happens to us will be good. Rather, we have been promised that all things, even the bad, will *work together* for our good in the end.

I love you all. We are all blessed. Our faith in Christ is stronger together!

We Need Each Other

It is week ten, and I have completed four of six treatments.

What a week! I knew the treatments would get more intense. "Endurance and faith. Endurance and faith." I keep saying it—and praying for it—over and over.

You know the old saying, "It's going to get worse before it gets better." I am living it. The good news is that my PSA numbers went from 49 to 30. Thank you, Lord. Our prayers are working, and I thank you all. I am humbled.

This was the first treatment where my body said, very insistently, "Rest," so I listened. I slept through most of it. As I slept, the chemo did its work, even without me being aware of it.

I was reminded of Psalm 145:3: "Great is the Lord, and greatly to be praised; and His greatness is unsearchable."

His greatness is limitless and incomprehensible. He is at work, doing far more than we realize. Just keep the faith. God never sleeps. He is always there. He hears our prayers. He forgives. He knows everything that we need, and He uses all of His resources to provide for us. He is love. So, as I sleep, I don't worry. I know the Lord loves me, even with all of my sins, weakness, and sickness. His love will never leave me.

The journey is getting tougher, and I am constantly reminded of how easy it would be to give in to fear, to start placing blame, to become negative. I won't do it. My faith won't allow it. Nice try, Satan!

Still, I know I must stay focused, so I pray for strength. No matter how tough the journey gets, I want to be someone who speaks wisely, who speaks life, who speaks truth, who speaks love. I hope others will see the greatness of our God through my example. I pray they will see that I am able to have peace of mind because of His constant provision.

I know the Lord is at work. He knows the plan. I just have to be patient, trusting that He is my path and He is my keeper as I journey through this dark valley. Through the Spirit, He enables us to see our many blessings even in the valleys. He teaches us through our hardships, and as a result, we become stronger in our faith.

God has provided me with so many resources for this journey, none more significant than the people in my life. I am so amazed and thankful for all of the people who support me, who share their prayers and wisdom, and who inspire me by living in a way that reflects the glory of God. The examples they provide give me inspiration for the journey.

My brothers and sisters, you've made such a positive impact on me. Your love and compassion for others is clear, and I thank you for walking with me. After all, the battle is not just about my faith vs. Satan's cancer. It's about all of us. The faith of each one of us is strengthened when we pray for each other. We are stronger together in Christ.

"Glory be to God, who by His mighty power at work within us is able to do far more than we would ever dare to ask or even dream of—infinitely beyond our highest prayers, desires, thoughts, or hopes." (Ephesians 3:20 TLB)

What I have learned through this journey, through all the prayers and support I have received, is that God created us for relationships. We need one another. He wants us to love and serve each other, so it is important that we place the needs of others on our hearts and in our prayers. God honors our prayers for one another, and I feel your prayers at work in me.

Whatever works against us—whether sickness or weakness—God is able.

As the prophet Isaiah said, "The LORD is the everlasting God, the Creator of the ends of the earth. He does not faint or grow weary; His understanding is unsearchable." (Isaiah 40:28)

The apostle Paul put it this way: "Oh, the depth of the riches both of the wisdom and knowledge of God! How unsearchable." (Romans 11:33)

I am thankful to God for His unfathomable greatness in every situation. In every struggle, we can simply ask the Holy Spirit to fill our hearts. He does not hide from us if we desire His presence.

Surrender, trust, and obey. His unfathomable greatness will provide all the resources you need. Thanks for your prayers. Thanks for placing me on your hearts. Thanks for being a resource of the Lord. I praise Him for all of you.

Bring the Rain

It's week eleven, and I am on the fourth of six treatments.

As my body takes in all of this chemo, I am feeling the side effects. I have become so weary. I know that a healing body going through chemo needs rest and a slower pace, so I'm trying to take it easy.

I see the PSA numbers dropping even as my hair keeps dropping (it's mostly gone by this point). The physical side of the battle is easy to understand: I go to treatment, I take a pill every day, the time-released medicine inside of me does its work. I can see, feel, and understand this.

It's the mental side of the battle that is harder to understand. Why does the fear blindside me sometimes? Why do those negative voices show up suddenly and try to create anxiety, even when they are not welcome? Why do I sometimes question the strength of my faith? Why do I sometimes ask the questions, "Why cancer? Why me? WHY ME?!"

Then I remember the story of the disciples in the storm. They were on a boat as the wind rose and the waves crashed, and they were terrified. But Jesus calmed their fears and stopped the storm.

I remember the time the disciples were unable to heal a man with leprosy. When they asked Jesus about this, he healed the man then told his disciples that they had failed due to a lack of faith.

What do these stories teach us? That we are weak, that we are sinners, and that we are prone to fear. If we want to conquer fear, we must remain in close relationship with the Lord and allow Him to continually strengthen our faith.

If the disciples who walked and talked with Jesus daily still had to struggle against fear and weakness, who am I to think I won't have these same struggles?

Realizing this, I refuse to beat myself up for my moments of fear. I know that all my strength comes from the Lord through the resources He provides, and it is my responsibility to be in a continuous and real relationship with Him. When the fear tries to set in, I must simply remember this and recommit myself.

It has become clear to me that the mental battle is the *real* battle. This is where I will win or lose. Even with all of the amazing advances in medical science, there remains an element of unpredictability in the physical battle because of the impact my attitude and emotions have on my physical well-being.

I believe it is possible for a patient to allow the mind to become so filled with fear, stress, doubt, and anger that it contributes to the body's illness. Remember, Satan is at work.

As I consider the mental battle, I am reminded of the lyrics from that song by Mercy Me:

> *Bring me joy, bring me peace*
>
> *Bring the chance to be free*
>
> *Bring me anything that brings You glory*
>
> *And I know there'll be days*

When this life brings me pain

But if that's what it takes to praise You

Jesus, bring the rain.

I am definitely feeling the rain, but I praise Jesus for bringing me closer to Him as a result.

"God calls weak ones and makes them strong ones so that their lives will constantly display His glory and the power of His grace." (Paul Tripp)

"It's not about believing Jesus walked on water. It's about knowing He is in the midst of your storm and He won't let you sink." (Tony Nolan)

My faith in Him *may* extend the length of my life. Even if it doesn't, I know that it has enhanced the *quality* of my life and gives me greater meaning and purpose.

"The Lord is near to all who call upon Him, to all who call upon Him in Truth." (Psalm 145: 18 NIV)

Thank you for being a resource God uses to strengthen others.

Let it rain.

God Is Enough

It's week twelve, and I am on the fourth of six treatments.

What a week! I've experienced so many blessings from family and friends. I am continually reminded that God is big enough for anything the world can dish out. I have so many praying for me, so many sending daily encouragements and words of wisdom. There is no better way to start the day than with words of true wisdom from the Lord. We all become greater in His greatness.

I need your prayers more than ever. Tomorrow, I begin treatment five of six. Again, it's all about faith and endurance.

Cancer is scary. It's hard to accept. It is troubling to know that the chemo is attacking both the bad and the good in my body. More than ever, I have to trust the Lord, but I am so thankful that you are all with me in this fight.

"Great beginnings are not as important as the way one finishes." (Dr. James Dobson)

I am going to finish this fight. I have never felt so strong or so loved, despite my weakened body.

"Be faithful in small things because it is in them that your strength lies." (Mother Theresa)

Yes, I see what Mother Theresa meant. Every day, there are small ways in which my faith is tested, and those small things make such a big impact on me. I pray I never lose clarity about that. When we are faithful in small things, God will trust us with bigger things.

In everything, the challenge is that God doesn't reveal His plan for us all at once. Instead, he takes us by the hand and leads us step by step into a future that only He can see—a future that may be bigger and more amazing than we could ever imagine. He is already preparing us for it. He is in control, so our future will unfold according to His will and in His time. We must simply hold on to His hand and trust Him.

Therefore, no matter what lies ahead, I pray that I will continue to trust and give thanks for everything. I am reminded of the time Jesus healed ten lepers:

"Then Jesus answered, 'Were not ten lepers cleansed? Where are the other nine? Was no one found to return and give praise to God except this foreigner?' And he said to him, 'Rise and go your way, your faith has made you well.'" (Luke 17:17-19 NIV)

Jesus healed ten, but only one understood that his healing was part of something bigger. Only one understood that Jesus was the very God who had healed him. He returned with thanksgiving, and he was saved by his faith.

I pray that I am always thankful for the blessings God has bestowed upon me. He has given me life, He has put wonderful brothers and sisters in my life, and He has a bigger plan for my life than I can ever imagine. I refuse to be one of the nine. I will continue to thank our Lord for everything He has done, even when I don't understand some of the twists and turns in my journey.

Thank you for your prayers and encouragement. As I keep saying, we are all stronger together in His greatness.

"For where two or three are gathered together in My name, I am there in the midst of them." (Matthew 18:20)

Answered Prayers

It's week thirteen, and my fifth treatment is done. Only one more to go.

My last treatment is scheduled for November 7, and my PSA number continues to drop. It's down to 25. Praise the Lord!

I'm sure your prayers for me have helped. During my last visit, the doctor did a double take when he walked into the room and saw me. He couldn't believe how good I looked. He said, "I'm amazed you're not curled up in the chair with weakness after everything we've put you through." As he made clear, the chemo they are giving me is bad stuff, but I have been mostly unaffected by the side effects. It's nothing more than answered prayers.

When I'm weak then I am strong through Him.

The doctor says my numbers are good, and the treatment seems to be working. Dr. Rosenfeld is such a great resource for the greatest healer of all: our Lord. As the doctor went through the list of all the side effects that most people experience with this kind of chemo (not a good list!), I realized how blessed I've been. The chemo has definitely slowed my body down, but your prayers are helping me stay ahead of the worst side effects. Thank you!

Though I truly do feel your prayers working in me, I also take responsibility for myself. As the old saying goes, "You can't pray for an A on a test but study for a B." I know I am weak and a sinner. I make mistakes, but I pray that God will help my actions match my prayers. I pray that I will continue to surrender, trust, and obey in all things.

One of you shared the following with me, so I want to share it with everyone. You called these the "Six Keys of Life."

Before I pray...I believe!

Before I speak...I listen!

Before I spend...I earn!

Before I write...I think!

Before I quit...I try!

Before I die...I live!

I have so much to be thankful for. First of all, I am thankful for this battle between my faith and Satan's cancer. Yes, I am thankful for it because it has made me a stronger person. As a result, I know I will be able to handle whatever lies ahead of me.

I am also thankful for all the resources God began to share with me as soon as Satan hit me with cancer. Life doesn't always make sense to us, but it always makes sense to God. Everything He allows fits perfectly into His plans, even if we don't know how. God wants us to use His resources, including His Holy Spirit and other people that He places along our path, so we can grow in our faith even in the midst of uncertainty.

When we are perplexed and don't know what to do, we must take comfort knowing that what is hidden to us is not hidden to Him. God is all powerful, all knowing, and He possesses *everything* we could ever need.

"The Lord is my light and my salvation—whom shall I fear? The Lord is the stronghold of my life—of whom shall I be afraid?" (Psalm 27:1 NIV)

"The people who know their God shall stand firm and take action." (Daniel 11:32b ESV)

It's Easy to Worry in Free Time

It is week fourteen. Treatment six is here—the last round of chemo!

In the battle of my faith vs. Satan's cancer, I am on the home stretch. I can tell you my body is weak, and I am scared. Even though I feel the prayers coming in daily—hourly—even though my faith has never been stronger, I can see and feel the weakness in my body. The chemo is compounding inside of me, and my body is demanding more and more rest. I am giving my body what it wants!

The physical weakness is easy to manage. When my body tells me to slow down, I slow down. However, I have never been good at being still. I prefer to be in the game. I love to work, to be around friends and family, to be outdoors, to *get stuff done.* I made the mistake years ago of letting Carla know this, and she is an expert at keeping me in motion (God has truly blessed me with her). Still, I can accept my body's changing needs.

The mental weakness is tougher. Being still can so easily lead to worrying. When my body is at rest, my mind wants to fill in the stillness, and I have to be careful about my thoughts going astray. All of this extra downtime is dangerous.

In the quiet moments, it is easy to start asking, "Why me?" It is easy to wonder, "Are the treatments really working?" It is easy to worry, "How much time do I have left to live?"

It is so easy to worry about *everything.*

Once your mind slips into that mode of worrying, then the anxiety takes hold. When that happens, you have to learn how to hit the brakes—I mean, lock the brakes up hard! If you let anxiety set in, Satan will start rampaging through your mind at full force. He wants you to blame everyone else, primarily God. He wants you to say, "I don't deserve this. It's not fair. God did this to me!" Blame leads to anger, and when the anger takes over, that's where Satan wins. He will get you completely wrapped up in blame and self-pity to the point of defeat.

I want to share with you something that was shared with me this week: "Jesus gave us 'Fear not' as a command, not a suggestion. Thou shalt not fear!"

To let fear consume us is to act as though Satan were bigger than God, but we know he isn't. We must remember continually that God is with us, and if God is with us, we have nothing to fear. Our faith should take the fear out of our lives. We know that God is in control, so why should we behave as if the devil were in control?

"So do not fear, for I am with you; do not be dismayed, for I am your God. I will strengthen you and help you; I will uphold you with my righteous right hand." (Isaiah 41:10 NIV)

In times of weakness and fear, I get my strength from God's greatness. Whatever journey you are on, fear not. God will never leave you nor forsake you. He has commanded you, "Fear not!" He is on your side.

"But I trust in you, O Lord; I say, 'You are my God.' My times are in your hand." (Psalm 31:14-15a NIV)

In the stillness, I will remember You, Lord. I will remind myself of all Your blessings. I will think about the many resources You have provided, including the brothers and sisters praying for me. We are all stronger together in You.

Learning What Cancer
Cannot Do

It is week fifteen, and the last chemo treatment is tomorrow.

In the battle between my faith and Satan's cancer, so many thoughts have been racing through my mind lately. These endless thoughts are wearing out my mind the same way that the chemo is wearing out my body. I know I've been a little grouchy, and I catch myself worrying about whether or not I will finish this battle strong. Will our prayers be answered? Will this battle end the way we all hope?

I just don't know, but all of this worrying is a reminder that I need to constantly turn my future over to the Lord. I will not allow Satan to sneak in and plant anxiety in my mind. My strength comes from my faith in the Lord, and I trust in all of His resources. Your prayers are at work, and my life is in His hands.

I've said it before, and I'll say it again. Nothing changes your life like hearing those three little words, "You have cancer." Since then, it feels like my life changes almost hourly.

As I get ready for the last treatment, I am committed to finishing strong. Cancer has changed so many things—in my body, in my mind, in my life—but there are some things that cancer *cannot* do.

It cannot diminish God's love for me. It cannot shatter my hope in Him. It cannot take my faith. It cannot destroy my peace. It cannot kill my friendships. It cannot suppress my memories. It cannot choose my attitude. It cannot steal eternal life. It cannot conquer my spirit.

Because of cancer, I have learned to deal with whatever is right in front of me. Instead of agonizing over the future, I take the next step and keep moving forward in faith.

This battle has been—and will always be—about my attitude and my faith. I am mindful of this verse:

"Be on guard; stand firm in the faith; be courageous; be strong." (1 Corinthians 16:13 NLT)

Fortunately, I don't stand alone. Family and friends help me maintain the right attitude. I keep coming back to what my friend Noah said, "Each of us is the source of the other, and our only strength is in knowing this."

To my friends and family, I thank you for being God's resource as I walk through this valley. You pray for me. You love me. You believe in me. You have cried with me. You have laughed with me (and *at* me). You share with me. You invest in me. You hold me accountable. You correct me. You teach me. You forgive me. You are always there for me!

I am so blessed!

Cancer might have come into my life to destroy me, but God has used it to teach me wisdom. Through cancer, he has shown me the love and support of my loved ones. He has taught me that my only strength comes from Him and His many resources. I have so much to be thankful for.

"I can do all things through Christ who gives me strength." (Philippians 4:13)

"Outside the will of God, there is nothing I want, and inside the will of God, there's nothing I fear!" (A.W. Tozer)

Sharing the Honey

The last treatment is done. Praise the Lord!

Today, as I was reading my daily devotional, I came across an old journal entry I had written. The devotional had asked me to paraphrase a proverb in my own words. I chose this proverb:

"It is not good to eat much honey; So to seek one's own glory is not glory." (Proverb 25: 27 NKJV)

This was my take on it:

When one spends much time on:

Trying to be promoted, trying to be noticed, trying to be loved, trying to be respected, trying to earn more, trying to buy more, trying to be forgiven—when all of your time is spent thinking about yourself, your efforts, what you have done—then you find yourself on a team of one.

You're only thinking about me, me, me. Little of value happens on a team of one. You need others to make things happen, so:

Focus on growing others. Focus on noticing others. Focus on promoting others. Focus on loving others. Focus on trusting others. Focus on respecting others. Focus on giving to others.

Focus on forgiving others. Focus on sharing with others. Focus on praying for others. Focus on loving others.

By being focused on investing in others and sharing God's love, true glory will be yours!

I thank you all for "sharing the honey" and investing in me. When we become a resource of God, we share in His true glory.

A True Test of Faith and Endurance

I was so excited and thankful to finish the last chemo treatment, but I think I got the cart before the horse. I was ready to get back to my normal life. I thought, "I've crossed the finish line! I'm back to the old Dan. Let's go!"

However, I have been quickly reminded that life doesn't always go the way we want. Yes, the last treatment is done, but the race is far from over. To my surprise, I have now found myself in the deepest valley in this journey. Life is full of surprises.

This week, I have been severely tested, both physically and mentally. There is not a single inch of my body that doesn't hurt. Even my fingernails and toenails ache. I have never felt weaker in my entire life. My muscles have almost no strength at all.

Mentally, I wasn't prepared for this pain. Because the treatments were done, I thought the worst was over. I failed to consider that the chemical cocktail they'd injected into my body is still there, and like all bad things, it takes time for its full effects to be felt. That's a life lesson right there. Yes, the bad that comes into your life never manifests fully right away. It enters your life, lurks in the dark for a while gathering strength, and finally strikes full force.

My faith and my attitude are being sorely tested—more than ever. As a result, Satan is knocking on the door again. He sees my physical and mental weakness as the perfect opportunity to stir up worry, fear, and doubt. He wants me to blame God. He wants me to start asking, "Why me? Why me? It's so unfair. What did I do to deserve this?" The devil would love nothing more than to see me overreact and let my faith falter. He would love to see me lie in my bed and fume: blaming God, blaming the doctors, blaming myself.

Well, not so fast, Satan.

"For everything that was written in the past was written to teach us, so that through the endurance taught in the Scriptures and the encouragement they provide we might have hope." (Romans 15:4 NIV)

As the valley deepens, I know God is still with me. He is still providing resources, still speaking to me through His Word, and He still has a plan. No valley is too deep for God!

"In the day when I cried out, you answered me, and made me bold with strength in my soul." (Psalm 138:3 NKJV)

No matter how deep the valley gets, I must *constantly* remind myself that everything is in His hands. When I am weak, He is strong. When I don't understand, I can trust that He does.

Still, I'm praying for the strength to trust and obey. I am praying that He will help me keep the negative voices at bay so His peace of mind can bring healing to my body.

"I can do all this through Him who gives me strength." (Philippians 4:13 NIV)

It is Thanksgiving week, and I have so much to be thankful for. No pain or weakness can choose my attitude for me or steal my faith. Walking through this deep valley will only make me stronger. No matter what lies ahead, His strength will be enough. I just remember this.

"In everything give thanks; for this is the will of God in Christ Jesus for you." (1 Thessalonians 5:18 NIV)

Thank you, Lord!

Keep Running the Race

It's week eighteen in the war between my faith and Satan's cancer.

In speaking to others who have battled cancer, I have been warned that the last chemo treatment has the longest recovery time. I am still so very weak. I pray this does indeed prove to be the last treatment, but I will have body scans on December 6.

I have written in the past few weeks about the importance of faith and endurance, but I am adding a new word to the list: **persistence**.

I have a picture on the wall above my desk of a Nebraska University football player from the year of Tom Osborne's first National Championship. Beneath the image, it says this:

"Persistence—The race goes not always to the swift but to those who keep running."

With cancer, there are so many hard knocks. It is a journey comprised of many races, so unless we persist in our faith, we're going to lose hope. God wants us to *live* in faith every step of the way. Sometimes, that is easier said than done. I often have to remind myself to *think less* and *pray more*.

"For as he thinketh in his heart, so is he." (Proverbs 23:7 KJV)

Endurance comes from knowing that the journey is going to be long and, at times, hard. It comes from praying and listening to the Lord, using all of his resources, including the doctors.

Persistence, on the other hand, is about *continuing to run* no matter the bumps in the road. You might not be able to run fast, but you can—you must—keep putting one foot in front of the other.

Remember, no matter what type of cancer you've got, no matter what stage you're at, someone has already gone on that journey before you and survived with their faith, hope, and joy intact.

"So do not fear, for I am with you; do not be dismayed, for I am your God. I will strengthen you and help you; I will uphold you with My righteous right hand." (Isaiah 41:10 NIV)

I will persist. I will keep running this race. By faith, I know the Lord is with me every step, and He will continue to uphold me with His right hand.

I turned one year older this week, and I was reminded of just how blessed I am. My daughter, Dani, came to visit for the weekend, and we watched the Shiloh football team advance to the state semifinals on Friday night.

It was a great birthday weekend full of family, football, friends, and so much faith. But the greatest blessing of all, and the greatest gift we have received, is the One and Only Son of our Heavenly Father—Jesus Christ—who came to save us.

It doesn't matter what we're going through, it doesn't matter how bad things are right now, because of Christ we have hope. Keep the faith. Surround yourself with friends and family and *keep running the race.*

"And let us run with perseverance the race marked out for us, fixing our eyes on Jesus, the pioneer and perfecter of faith." (Hebrews 12:1b-2 NIV)

I will not accept defeat, because God always leads me in Christ's triumphal procession.

Determined to Finish Strong

It is week nineteen in the war between my faith and Satan's cancer.

I am praying for God's will to be done and trusting that His will is good. In my battle with cancer, as I've said before, I am learning that it is not one race but many races—as it is with life. I now know that I will be running these races for the rest of my life. They are a part of me. Through faith, endurance, and persistence, I have to keep running. No matter the circumstances I encounter along the way, I must stay focused on the One who controls it all.

I surrender, trust, and obey, so that "my joy may remain in you, and that your joy may be full." (John 15:11b NKJV)

As I am running these many races, I keep reminding myself that "there is a time for everything and a season for every activity under the heavens." (Ecclesiastes 3:1 NIV)

No matter how tough the road ahead may look, or how weak my body feels, I know God is with me, and He will help me continue to put one foot in front of the other—to persist. In the end, His desire will prevail. I am not big enough, but He is. God has the perspective of eternity, while my vision is limited and my understanding finite. Therefore, in everything, I pray for His will to be done.

My body scans are scheduled for next week, and it will be the start of a whole new race in this battle with cancer. Fortunately, I feel a little better every day. I have so many prayers strengthening me. Life is a team sport. We need each other to keep running the race.

I've learned so much on this journey, but above all, I am learning how to follow God day by day. Cancer is not the destination, merely a tactic of Satan in his endless attempts to turn me against God. He will not succeed.

The destination is Jesus. Everything is meant to move me closer to Him, so I must be mindful of that with every step I take. Fortunately, His Word and His resources are there to guide me. Sometimes, we just have to slow down for a bit and look up. God gives us many signs along the way, and we'll see them if we're looking to Him instead of obsessing over how hard the road is.

No matter what, have faith and keep running whatever race you are in. God will get you where you need to go. No matter what happens after my scans next week, no matter what the new race looks like, I know I have been—and will continue to be—very blessed. I won't run the new race alone, and I won't forget that my true destination is Jesus.

Keep the faith, stay in the race, and finish strong, trusting in His Word and His resources. Persist!

Thankful for the Greatest Gift

In all journeys of life, we have to remember to stay in motion no matter how steep the hill is in front of us. We are blessed with different seasons, some harder than others, so keep moving. Things will get better, but look for the good no matter how hard the next step is. Keep your faith, family, and friends close in all seasons.

Speaking of seasons, Christmas is drawing near, and the joy of the holiday season is all around us. Unbelievable blessings can be seen everywhere. After all, we are celebrating the greatest gift ever: Jesus. Thank you, Lord God, for the gift of Your one and only Son.

This time of year, it is so important to celebrate His birth, remember His perfect life, His teachings, and the horrific death that He suffered for our sins, conquering death by rising on the third day. Because of this, we have also received His gift of the Holy Spirit. And *that* gift is always with us, in every breath we take, in every thought we have, in every step we take.

Since it is a season of giving, don't forget to open your heart fully to Him. That is the greatest gift we can give to God. Receive the Holy Spirit fully. No matter what journey you're on, no matter how hard the road is in front of you, He will never leave you.

One of the great joys of Christmas is seeing kids unwrap their gifts. Remember what it was like when you were young? Remember the excitement and joy on Christmas morning as you gazed in wonder at all the presents under the tree? There is nothing quite like it. That's the attitude we should have toward the Lord and His many gifts for us.

"Whoever humbles himself like this child is the greatest in the kingdom of heaven." (Mathew 18:4 ESV)

There's a reason why Jesus always made time for children. Even when others tried to keep them away, He said, "No, let them come to me!" He wants us to learn from their example, to have the same excitement in our faith that children have on Christmas morning.

I want to live with that kind of excitement every day, full of joy and gratitude for every gift He gives me. In this journey, cancer is now at rest in my body, and I am feeling better every day. This, too, is a gift from God. I am very blessed.

Speaking of gifts, a friend of mine said something rather surprising to me once. He told me he received one of the best gifts ever on his fortieth birthday.

"What was it?" I asked.

"Cancer," he replied.

He is a few years past forty, so this was a while ago. Since then, he has won his fight against cancer, and he's doing well these days, by the grace of God. However, when he said it was one of the best gifts he'd ever received, I thought he was nuts! Cancer is from Satan, and who wants a gift from him?

Today, I understand exactly what my friend meant. The gift wasn't really the cancer. No, Satan's cancer comes to only to steal, kill, and destroy. When I learned I had cancer, I found myself in a daily battle for my life. But it brought out the fight in me, and it taught me what it truly means to walk by faith. That was the real gift—the journey with Him.

Cancer awakened the Holy Spirit's presence in my life. It revealed to me the true power of God and all of His resources. It showed me the power of prayer, faith, family, and friends. Satan has thrown his best at me, and he failed. He lost. He didn't drive me away from God. He only pushed me closer.

"Not only that, but we rejoice in our sufferings, knowing that suffering produces endurance, and endurance produces character, and character produces hope, and hope does not put us to shame, because God's love has been poured into our hearts through the Holy Spirit who has been given to us." (Romans 5: 3-5 ESV)

Jesus isn't like the gifts we receive on Christmas morning because He doesn't come around once a year. He is like a joyful season that never ends. I am so thankful for all He has done for us, all He will do for us, by His grace. I thank Him for my life, and I entrust my life to Him.

Merry Christmas. Enjoy the journey. Thank you for being part of mine.

Blessed and Thankful

The battle between my faith and Satan's cancer continues, but I am feeling so much better these days. Even my hair is coming back. It's a lot grayer now and really fuzzy, but at least it's there—a sign of a new beginning.

It's a new year as well, and so much has changed. No more chemo. I am getting some of my strength back, and I am able to do more. I still need your prayers because the cancer is still inside of me. The negative voices still want to whisper in my ear and weaken me, so I have to stay focused on Him.

God says, "Do not remember the former things, nor consider the things of old. Behold, I will do a new thing." (Isaiah 43: 18-19 NKJV)

As we move into a new year, it's a brand-new start for me. My faith has never been stronger. As a result of my battle with cancer, I have experienced the power of prayer, so I head into this year with greater confidence than ever.

I was recently told that 37 percent of people with cancer eventually die from the disease. I don't know if that's accurate. You hear so many different "statistics" about cancer when you're battling it. Some of those statistics can be discouraging, and you never know quite what to believe. Still, even if it's true, that means 63 percent survive. Those aren't bad odds. No matter what my chances are, I have made my choice to accept God's will, whatever it is.

Maintaining a positive attitude is key. I have to keep the faith, and I have to keep my family and friends close. This is not a one-time choice. It is a choice I make every hour of every day. I must continue to use the resources God has blessed me with, and I must choose—every moment—to surrender, trust, and obey.

God loves me, but Satan is alive and he attacks every day. At every turn, he wants to push me farther from God. Therefore, in the new year, I resolve to pray more and listen more to my Lord.

"Ask and it will be given to you; seek and you will find, knock and the door will be opened to you." (Matthew 7:7 NIV)

In every situation, I have to ask, seek, and knock. The Lord will provide what I need to overcome any and every tactic of Satan.

Remember, we are all resources of the Lord for one another. Sometimes, we are the answer to another person's prayer. Therefore, let's all commit to responding faithfully to Him this year, and let us be mindful of Satan's lies, discouragements, and temptations.

No matter what the new year holds, I know life isn't always fair, but what we make of it is up to us. Surround yourself with God and His resources. Maintain a positive attitude, a fighting spirit, during both the good days and the bad. Satan lurks around every corner, but Jesus walks right beside us all the way. We do not fight alone.

"I can do all things through Christ who strengthens me." (Philippians 4:13 NIV)

"Look to the Lord and His strength; seek his face always." (Psalm 105:4 NIV)

Sometimes, in looking to the Lord and trusting His strength, I just have to get out of the way. I can't always trust myself because I am weak and a sinner, but I can always trust Him. Satan wants me to worry. He wants me to feel unworthy. He wants to bring sin into my life. I must not allow it.

"Forgetting what lies behind and straining forward to what lies ahead, I press on toward the goal for the prize of the upward call of God in Christ Jesus." (Philippians 3:13b-14 ESV)

In Jesus, we have our greatest example of perfect love, perfect joy, perfect peace, perfect patience, perfect kindness, perfect goodness, perfect faithfulness, perfect gentleness, perfect forgiveness, perfect wisdom, and perfect strength.

Let's make it our goal to be more like Jesus in the year ahead. The Holy Spirit lives in us. He is the one who transforms us, making us more like Jesus as we surrender to Him daily.

Stay strong, for He is always with us.

Being Before Doing

I continue to feel better every day, but I know there will always be good and bad days. Every step of our journey is important, whether we are walking on solid ground or sliding down into another valley.

"The grass withers, the flower fades, but the word of our God stands forever." (Isaiah 40:8 NASB)

In my fight with cancer, I've definitely had some very bad days, days when I felt my faith faltering, when the ground beneath my feet seemed shaky. It would have been so easy on those days to fall, but somehow the Lord kept me going.

"As for me, I will always have hope; I will praise more and more." (Psalm 71:14 NIV)

We don't always have a choice about where our next step will take us, what the ground will be like, or where the road ahead leads, but God knows. So, no matter what this day brings, whether good or bad, even as Satan's cancer lies dormant within me, I will trust the Lord and His resources. It was not my choice to have cancer. In fact, I didn't get any say in the matter. However, it *is* my choice to pray every day that God will help me surrender, trust, and obey Him.

"As for God, His way is perfect; the word of the Lord is proven; He is a shield to all who trust in Him." (2 Samuel 22:31 NKJV)

Sometimes, I wonder what this journey would have been like if I didn't trust the Lord. I truly believe that without my faith, family, and friends, this journey would have had a quick ending.

There's always a chance that my next step will be into quicksand, so I take nothing for granted. I know that the key to my survival thus far has been less about *doing* and more about *being*. In my weakest moments, it was *being* in love with the Lord that carried me through.

Although I pray that the Holy Spirit will move me to take action in sharing God's love, I understand that it all starts with *being*. Being before doing—that makes life so much easier. Being in love with our Lord no matter where our next step takes us—that's the key.

"Love never fails!" (1 Corinthians 13:8 NIV)

Strengthening My Faith

This week, in the battle between my faith and Satan's cancer, I went back to the doctor for a second injection of a time-release drug that will last for six months. It is supposed to keep the prostate cancer at rest inside of me. I also take a pill once a day that works in tandem with the injection.

My doctors are a great resource that God has provided me to fight the physical side of the cancer. One injection every six months and one pill a day? I can handle this. With God's help, the physical side is winning.

As always, the real fight is on the mental side. Where is the time-release faith booster that can be injected into my mind to keep the doubt, fear, and temptation at bay for the next six months?

I know others have gone before me on the cancer journey, and I know there are many other kinds of burdens that people are carrying on their own journeys. Satan has a way of piling on. He will throw as much at us as he is able to throw. Remember the example of Job!

In the absence of a time-release faith booster, I do find ways to bolster my faith during the dark days. First, I have to be willing to talk about my struggles. Satan thrives in the darkness. When I open up, admit I'm weak, and talk about my journey with others, my faith is strengthened. None of us can fight our battle alone. If we try, we will lose. Satan is stronger than any individual person.

Therefore, we must be willing to rely on *all* the resources that God provides us along the way. With every step, we must look to Him—surrender, trust, and obey.

Life isn't fair, and no one is perfect. We need each other. We are each other's faith booster. Do you notice the people around you who are struggling to carry their burdens? Have you allowed yourself to become one of God's faith boosters in their lives?

I have been fortunate to have friends and family who help me carry the burden of cancer. They don't allow my faith to become sidelined by the hardships on this journey. Like them, I want to help others who are struggling.

"Bear one another's burdens, and so fulfill the law of Christ." (Galatians 6:2 ESV)

Be bold enough to share your burdens with others. God has placed people around you to help you carry them, if you're willing to open up. At the same time, be ready and willing to help those around you in their time of need. This is what we are all called to.

"So now I am giving you a new commandment: Love each other. Just as I have loved you, you should love each other." (John 13:34 NLT)

To help others, we must be guided by the Lord's wisdom. We must be careful not to:

Compare ourselves with others.

Compete with others.

Criticize others.

Arrogance, pride, and envy get in the way. If we aren't led by the Lord's wisdom, we can do more harm than good in trying to help others. Remember, Satan is always looking for a way to cause trouble.

"So, if you think you are standing firm, be careful that you don't fall!" (1 Corinthians 10:12 NIV)

"This is my prayer: that your love may abound more and more in knowledge and depth of insight." (Philippians 1:9 NIV)

"God is love." (1 John 4:16 NIV)

"Let all that you do be done in love." (1 Corinthians 16:14 ESV)

Making the Right Choices

I feel so much better these days that I'm shocked. Through six rounds of chemo, my PSA went from over 1,400 to 4.9 (yes, that is four-point-nine)! What a blessing. All glory to God and the power of His resources.

"God is our refuge and strength, a very present help in trouble." (Psalm 46:1 KJV)

At the beginning of this journey, I was in real trouble. As soon as I heard those three simple words, "You have cancer," the reality of death hit me hard and fast, yet, ironically, it also showed me how to truly live.

God enables us to choose how we respond to any and every situation. Frankly, I've made some terrible choices in my life. However, the best choice I ever made was to confess that I'm weak and a sinner in need of help, entrusting my life to Jesus, my Savior. In my time of trouble, I chose to put my faith in God and all His resources. Making that choice sounds easier than it actually was. The negative voices are always there to cloud our decisions. They tempt us, deceive us, discourage us, and make what should be an easy choice far more difficult. Even our small wrong choices can cause us a lot of trouble.

What made me think I could choose to maintain my faith during the fight of my life? What made me think I could defeat Satan and all of his deceptions? The odds were stacked against me. Except for God. Because of Him, the odds were always in my favor. I **chose** to trust His will. I **chose** to be open and share my journey with others. I **chose** to stay positive. I **chose** to listen to loved ones. I **chose** to spend my time wisely, feeding my faith instead of my doubt and fear.

"You will recognize them by their fruits. Are grapes gathered from thorn bushes, or figs from thistles?" (Matthew 7:16 ESV)

When your journey heads into a deep valley, when thorn bushes and thistles appear on your path, don't let them distract you. Don't let the negative cloud your judgment. If you allow the negative to inform your choices, you will head down the wrong path. Surround yourself with God's resources, hold onto your faith, and the right path will be clear.

Even when we fall short, we are still loved and forgiven. Choose to surrender, trust, and obey in every circumstance. Choose to trust His resources, and choose to *be* one of His resources. We are stronger together. Even the smallest choices matter. If you can choose wisely in the small moments, then choosing wisely in the big moments will come easier.

Remember, with God all things are possible.

His Love Will Get You Through

It feels good to feel good. More than that, it feels good to win! This week, one of God's great resources, Dr. Rosenfeld, called me. He talked about my cancer to Dr. Robert Dreiser at the University of Virginia, and they believe I should try a treatment called PROVENGE.

PROVENGE is an advanced, proactive immunotherapy for prostate cancer. Apparently, there are no side effects, and I would only require three treatments. I'm all in! They are setting up my appointments in Tulsa.

Feeling good now reminds me of just how weak I felt at my lowest point. Looking back, it has become crystal clear just how close I came to losing this battle. It's amazing how quickly Satan can change your whole life. When we think we're strong, he sees our real weakness, and that's when he strikes.

No matter how good things are going for you right now, the battle of your life might be just around the corner. While this shouldn't make us worry constantly, it should make us mindful of every step we take. Cancer hits hard. Finding out you have it will bring even the strongest man to his knees.

One day, I was living my "normal" life, and the next day, I was headed down into the deepest valley of my life. And it all changed when I heard those three little words, "You have cancer." The path felt like it went straight down, and I remember wondering, "How far down can I possibly fall? How weak can I get? How will I survive?"

"Now faith, hope, and love abide, these three; but the greatest of these is love." (1 Corinthians 13:13 ESV)

Faith, hope, and love. In the end, that's what it all comes down to. It really is that simple, even when you're in the fight of your life.

I have never forgotten an early Sunday School lesson I learned. My teacher asked us the question, "Who or what should you love the most?"

My hand went straight up. I knew this one! Confident, I answered, "Dad and Mom!"

Many of the kids agreed with me, but the teacher shook her head. "To truly love others," she said, "you have to love God first. Why? Because God *is* love. All that is good comes from His love. We are able to truly love others because of our love for Him."

In my deepest valley, I learned what that old Sunday School lesson means.

"Every valley shall be filled, and every mountain and hill shall be made low, and the crooked shall become straight, and the rough places shall become level ways." (Luke 3:5 ESV)

By loving God, my crooked path through the valley was made straight, and the road that looked too rough was made level. My love for Him carried me through my worst days and enabled me to continue to love and hope, even when I had almost no strength left in my body.

"And it is my prayer that your love may abound more and more, with knowledge and all discernment." (Philippians 1:9 ESV)

No matter how good things are going in your life right now, remember that there are no mountains without a valley. Keep growing in your knowledge and understanding of God, and dive deeper in His love. Then you'll be ready for whatever you find around the next bend in the road. Don't fear. On the day you enter your deepest valley, you will learn that God's love is all-powerful, so always give thanks in every circumstance.

No matter where your journey takes you, His love will get you through. His love always wins in the end.

Hope Is a Choice

The battle continues between my faith and Satan's cancer.

Another thing I've learned in the fight for my life: happiness is available even in our deepest valleys because our true happiness is a fruit of God's love.

"Behold, the eye of the Lord is on those who fear him, on those who hope in His steadfast love." (Psalm 33:18 ESV)

During the worst days of my cancer journey, I cried so many tears they seemed to have no end. Most of those tears were shed when I had to tell my family about the diagnosis, but I will never forget how we rallied our faith in that moment. We took a huge step forward as a family when we decided to trust God, and I pray we never lose that feeling.

As terrible as it was to learn I had cancer, I now realize what it has done for my family. We have more confidence in the Lord. We know now that we can handle anything Satan dreams up because the Lord is with us.

Through all the tears and hugs, the Holy Spirit brought us together like never before. To this day, I still remember the power we felt in that moment. Even though Satan's cancer had entered my body, we chose to believe that Satan would not control *us*.

Our love for each other became stronger than ever, and as a result, we became stronger in Him. Instead of crumbling under the weight of fear, we turned to prayer, asking the Lord for wisdom, direction, confidence, acceptance, and healing.

"Is anyone among you suffering? Let him pray. Is anyone cheerful? Let him sing praise." (James 5:13 ESV)

We made the choice to respond to cancer with faith, and it has made all the difference. On that day, when we accepted His will and shared our faith with one another, we took our first step out of that deep valley.

No matter what happens to you, God enables you to make the choice to trust in His love, to trust in His resources, to put your hope in Him. We could have gone the other way, we could have become angry, fearful, and bitter toward God, but we didn't. I could have shaken my fist at the sky and said, "How dare you do this to me!" What a different road it would have been if I had!

That is exactly what the negative voices wanted me to do, but I didn't listen. I chose to trust God and His resources to get me through this fight. We all face this choice during times of trouble. Will you turn *toward* God or *away* from God in your deepest valley? That is a choice you have to make.

"But may the righteous be glad and rejoice before God; may they be happy and joyful." (Psalm 68:3 NIV)

The joy of the Lord is always available to you, no matter what you're going through. In your time of trouble, He will enable you to choose faith over fear, trust over doubt, acceptance over blame. Accept that you are weak and needy. Turn to Him. Hand your life, your future, and all your outcomes to Him. Be willing to lean on all the resources He places around you, including friends and family. When you do, you will find happiness, even on your darkest days.

"Let love and faithfulness never leave you; bind them around your neck, write them on a tablet of your heart." (Proverbs 3:3 NIV)

"Your love, Lord, reaches to the heavens, your faithfulness to the skies." (Psalm 36:5 NIV)

God has a plan for us. Are we willing to trust Him, even if that plan takes us to some difficult places? As for me, I pray every day that His will be done. I pray that the Lord will fill me with the Holy Spirit and give me the strength to surrender, trust, and obey in every circumstance.

Choose hope, choose to trust Him, no matter what Satan throws at you.

My Faith vs. Me? Can It Be?

"Many are the plans in a person's heart, but it is the Lord's purpose that prevails." (Proverbs 19:21 NIV)

When you learn you have cancer, one of the hardest things to handle is the complete interruption of your plans. No, I never anticipated having cancer, never would have wanted it, and certainly didn't plan for it. Prior to that first doctor's appointment, I didn't even know what PSA (prostate-specific antigen) was. In one day, in one *hour*, in one *minute*, I found myself in the fight of my life, and I wasn't prepared for the interruption!

I had everything planned out already. Life was going well. I was on a great path. Why did cancer have to come in and bring it all to a screeching halt? I struggled to accept it. I wanted the Lord to take it away and restore me immediately to my plans.

However, as He often does, the Lord allowed this hardship to remind me of who is truly in control and whose purpose will prevail. His plans for us are always the best. Sometimes, I get in my own way. I try to fight God's will. I refuse the plans He has for me.

He opens a door and says, "Go this way," and I reply, "No, Lord, not that way. That way looks too hard. I don't have time for it. I am choosing a different direction."

If we're not careful, we can end up wasting a lot of time and energy trying to avoid the path that the Lord has chosen for us. I have to constantly remind myself that God has a plan for me—He has *always* had a plan for me.

Even if you don't like the look of the path the Lord has prepared for you, have faith and remember that He will be with you every step of the way. Every door the Lord opens, every curve and bend in the path, has some purpose, even if we can't understand it. Seek His wisdom and keep moving forward.

"Your word is a lamp to my feet and a light to my path." (Psalm 119:105 ESV)

Sometimes, God opens a door, and we try hard to close it. Other times, He closes a door, and we work hard to force it open. So much unhappiness comes from fighting against His will for our lives.

"But it's not what I wanted," we say. "It's not what I planned. It's not what I expected."

Put your life fully in His hands. Trust that He knows best. Trust that He has a great purpose for your life, even in hardship and suffering. Don't get in your own way! Let the Lord's will be done.

"Thus, you will walk in the ways of the good and keep to the paths of the righteous." (Proverbs 2:20 NIV)

A door you never expected to go through might swing open one day and hit you right in the face. The path beyond that door might head straight down into the deepest valley of your life. Still, God wouldn't call you to move that way if He didn't intend to give you all the resources you need to get through it.

"My son, if you accept My words and store up My commands within you, turning your ear to wisdom and applying your heart to understanding—indeed, if you call out for insight and cry aloud for understanding, and if you look for it as for silver and search for it as for hidden treasure, then you will understand the fear of the LORD and find the knowledge of God." (Proverbs 2:1-5 NIV)

Cancer was a door that swung open and hit me right in the face, but I ultimately chose to trust God and follow His path. I refused to blame God, to shake my fist at him and shout, "It's not fair. It's not fair," but to trust that He knew what He was doing. The path of blame, anger, and doubt leads to ruin. You don't want to go that way!

Accept the door that God has opened in front of you, no matter how bad it seems. He knows what He is doing, and He has the best plan for your life.

"I can do all this through Him who gives me strength." (Philippians 4:13 NIV)

I had an appointment at Highlands Oncology today—another one of God's great resources—and learned that my PSA has dropped from 4.92 to 3.45. The doctor said my bone marrow looked as healthy as a horse! God is in control. I trust His plans for my life!

"'For My thoughts are not your thoughts, neither are your ways My ways,' declares the Lord. 'As the heavens are higher than the earth, so are My ways higher than your ways and My thoughts than your thoughts.'" (Isaiah 55:8-9 NIV)

No matter what the future holds in store, I know who wins in the end. The Lord has already declared victory.

"'I am the Alpha and the Omega,' says the Lord God, 'Who is, and Who was, and Who is to come, the Almighty.'" (Revelation 1:8)

What My Opponent
Taught Me

Satan's intention was to destroy my faith, but I have only become stronger in this battle. I have learned so much from my opponent. No matter how smart, how important, how big, or how strong we think we are, we are all weak, and we are all sinners, and we desperately need God's help.

We don't fully realize this until we go up against an enemy who is too powerful for us. Everyone faces an insurmountable obstacle at some point. Without faith, it can be devastating. It can be the point of no return. However, when we turn fully to God, trusting Him and His resources, no enemy is too great. We are stronger in Him, so when the enemy comes against you, go *all in*. That means learning from His Word, relying on His resources, and trusting in His will.

As I've said, faith is not believing that God *can*, it is knowing that God *will*. He has already declared that your life will be victorious, so what are you afraid of? My opponent taught me how to truly trust the Lord, no matter my circumstances. He also taught me that I do not fight alone. I turned to my friends and family, and their prayers and support made me so much stronger.

"I long to see you so that I may impart to you some spiritual gift to make you strong—that is, that you and I may be mutually encouraged by each other's faith." (Romans 1:11-12 NIV)

The enemy came to steal, kill, and destroy, but God used Satan's evil intentions to make me stronger. None of us have to fight alone. With our mutual faith and hope, all bound up in God's love for us, we will win every battle!

"And now these three remain: faith, hope and love. But the greatest of these is love." (1 Corinthians 13:13 NIV)

We are stronger together because of His love. I pray the Lord will give each of us courage to see His purpose in every circumstance. Ask for His wisdom to help you understand His will in the midst of the enemy's schemes. Remember, God is love. You are never alone!

Strength and Wisdom for Each Day

I'm spending a beautiful Spring Break week with my family in Cabo at the invitation of my sister and brother-in-law. We're having a great time. The last time I went on vacation was last July when I got my cancer diagnosis, and what a difference!

That July, my mind was filled day and night with questions. "How will Carla and I tell the kids about my cancer? How will they react? What am I going to do? How will I survive?" It was not the ideal way to enjoy a vacation. We spent the week desperately praying, trying to take it one day at a time, knowing our faith was going to be tested like never before.

"Call upon me in the day of trouble; I will deliver you, and you shall glorify me." (Psalm 50:15 ESV)

We *did* call upon the Lord, day after day. The prayers were like a tidal wave, sweeping over everything else. However, God taught us to trust Him. He strengthened our faith and helped us keep moving forward.

I know the battle isn't over, but I feel like I am slowly climbing out of this deep valley. For that, I give God the glory. He held my hand and guided me through my toughest battles, and He provided so many resources along the way to keep my faith strong.

Now, He has blessed me with this beautiful view of the ocean here in Cabo. What a gift! The ocean, the sand, the palm trees, the warm sun—it's all so relaxing. On this vacation, we are celebrating life and the power of faith. Surrounded by all of this beauty, I feel so close to God. He is good, and I trust Him.

The Bible says, "Seek the LORD while he may be found; call on Him while he is near." (Isaiah 55:6 ESV)

My perspective on all of my battles is so much clearer now. As I look back at every hardship I've endured in my life, I realize how the Lord used each of those situations to turn my heart toward him. Everything that happens has some greater purpose. There are always lessons God wants us to learn, even if we can't understand at the time. In faith, however, we can trust Him even when His purpose isn't yet clear. Someday, we will know.

Long before I learned I had cancer, God was using His Word and His resources to prepare me for the fight of my life. Since then, He continues to use them to strengthen my faith and to help me grow in wisdom.

I now understand that no matter my earthly circumstances, whether I'm in good health or bad, I am desperately in need of God every day. We are all in dire need of Him at every stage of our journey, even if we don't realize it. Though I feel like I'm on the upward slope, I need Him just as much now as I ever did. I must continue to walk in love and trust.

"A wise person thinks a lot about death, while a fool thinks only about having a good time." (Ecclesiastes 7:4 NLT)

Having cancer has made me a better person. Cancer made me think a lot about death, but confronting my own mortality taught me how to truly live. It made me rely more on my faith, family, and friends. I now cherish every second, and I take nothing for granted. I am truly blessed for every moment God gives me.

We never know what tomorrow holds. Surround yourself with God and His resources because only He knows what is next, whether good or bad. You don't know what Satan will hit you with, so walk in readiness. God knows, and He will prepare you for the next battle.

Don't wait until desperation drives you to seek the Lord. Don't wait until you're in a time of need. Seek the Lord now. Build your faith in good days and bad. Always remember, He is our deliverer, our salvation, our conqueror. He loves us every day, and He knows the road ahead. He will be with you on good days and bad, on the mountaintop and in the deepest valley.

"The LORD is my rock and my fortress and my deliverer, my God, my rock, in whom I take refuge, my shield, and the horn of my salvation, my stronghold." (Psalm 18:2 ESV)

Suffering Is Helping Me
Fix Myself

I have been amazed at how much faith grows in a time of trials, but only when we understand—and accept—God's real purpose in them. I received great advice from a Christian brother in the midst of a trial a few years ago. I've never forgotten it.

I had just finished recounting all of my problems, all of the things I was worried about, including some people who I felt had wronged me, when he said, "Don't worry about that. Don't worry about them. Just fix yourself!"

At first, his statement set me back.

I thought, "Did you not just hear what I said? Did you not just hear what they did to me?"

Fortunately, I didn't say this out loud. Instead, I considered his statement, prayed about it, slept on it, and prayed some more. In the end, I realized he was right. No matter what I'm going through, the best response is always to *fix myself*.

It is easy to cast blame: on others, on God, on circumstances beyond our control. It is much harder to admit our own mistakes, our faults, and our own areas of needed improvement, but suffering makes it easier to see those faults and implement changes in our lives. After all, gold is a lot easier to shape and mold when it's heated in the furnace.

This is a long-term project for me. I keep working on improving myself every day. To make progress, I need help from the people closest to me, because they help me see what I need to change in myself. As I strive to become the best person I can be, I need their advice, prayers, encouragement, and accountability. This is why I keep saying, "We are stronger together in Him."

What a blessing my friends, family, church, and men's group have been. They strengthen me and help me grow in so many ways. We are not meant to face our battles alone. God uses other people. We can't afford to isolate ourselves.

"Where there is no guidance, a people falls, but in an abundance of counselors there is safety." (Proverbs 11:14 ESV)

On the other hand, you have to be careful whom you lean on. Some people will bring out the worst in you. They will get you to focus on how others have wronged you. They will turn your heart and mind to revenge. They will turn you from God and get you worked up over the unfairness of life. All of this is a massive waste of time. More than that, it's a road that leads to ruin!

Yes, life is unfair, and sometimes people hurt us, but God wants us to grow, change, improve, and become more like Jesus. Flee from the "us vs. them" mentality.

"Do not be deceived: Bad company ruins good morals." (1 Corinthians 15:33 ESV)

Lean on friends and family who will strengthen your faith and encourage you. Entrust yourself to those who will speak the truth in love to you. As God reveals your areas of needed growth, let Him begin to change you in positive ways.

I can't control what other people do. I can only control myself, so no matter what I go through, I choose to **fix myself** and **forgive others**. It's not easy, but the trials in life make the job of self-repair easier. They have made it clear what a "fixer-upper" I am, but they have also taught me to rely on God's help.

"He whose ear listens to the life-giving reproof will dwell among the wise. He who neglects discipline despises himself, but he who listens to reproof acquires understanding. The fear of the LORD is the instruction for wisdom, and before honor comes humility." (Proverbs 15:31-33 NASB)

Jesus was a carpenter in life. He is a carpenter of *people* now. He knows how to repair our brokenness! Every day, I pray that the Lord will help me become a better Christian, a better husband, a better father, a better son, a better brother, a better friend, a better leader, and a better worker. I want to be a great resource in Him for others, and I accept my responsibility for implementing needed changes in me.

"A wise man will hear and increase in learning, and a man of understanding will acquire wise counsel." (Proverbs 1:5 NASB)

Even if we can't see how all of the dots connect, we can choose to believe that God will use every trial to shape us and help us grow. When I go through trials now, I look back and remember how the Lord has taught me, strengthened me, and blessed me during some of the worst times in my life.

On the other hand, when we fight against the Lord's will, when we rage about life's unfairness, we just sink deeper into despair. It's like quicksand. The secret to getting out of quicksand is to stop thrashing, calm down, and look for the resources around you that can help you get out. When you calm down and turn to the Lord, He will begin to show you the resources He has placed around you. He never expected you to face this trial alone.

Look for His will in every situation. What is He trying to teach you? What areas of needed improvement is He revealing to you?

Don't focus on how others have wronged you or how unfair life is. Instead, trust the Lord and His path for you. It leads to eternal life.

The Foundation of Faith Is Love

Before our vacation, Carla tore all three tendons in her hamstring completely off the bone. The doctor was amazed that she was even able to walk. They drained 30cc of blood, gave her a cortisone injection, then sent us on our way to Cabo. She still managed to have a great time, but she finally had surgery to repair the torn tendons this week.

I also had another procedure this week. They inserted a tunnel catheter in my neck in preparation for the new PROVENGE treatments that will start on April 14th. It wasn't a good time, believe me. I hate being awake in the operating room! I wish I was as tough as Carla. She handles surgical procedures much better than I.

Life is so crazy sometimes. Trouble just doesn't wait for a convenient moment. Carla and I had no time in our lives for all of these medical problems, but they happened anyway. All we can do is pray and roll with it. Thankfully, our faith provides us the strength to get through each day, no matter how crazy.

Carla's recovery from surgery is going to be long and hard. Fortunately, I am feeling good enough these days to attend to her needs, as she has attended to my needs in the past. These hardships have made our love for each other stronger than ever.

My older daughter, Dani, is in town. She extended her stay in order to help us. My niece, Ashley, has also been a huge supporter. I keep saying it. "Turn to your loved ones in a time of trouble." They are God's resources. Don't try to fight your battles alone. God is love, and He surrounds us with love if we are willing to receive it. I can't imagine my life without my friends and family. I am so humbled.

My PSA numbers dropped again, from 3.45 to 2.55. Thank you, Lord. That is some good news in the midst of a crazy week.

Good news or bad, I know my well-being rests on God's love, strength, and wisdom. He is always *with* us, and He is always *for* us. God's love for us and our love for Him—this is the unshakeable foundation we can stand on in any situation. Our hope starts and ends right there. Remember, Jesus was asked by one of the Pharisees, "Which is the greatest commandment in all of the Laws?"

"Jesus replied: 'Love the Lord your God with all your heart and with all your soul and with all your mind.' This is the first and greatest commandment. And the second is like it: 'Love your neighbor as yourself.' All the Law and the Prophets hang on these two commandments.'" (Matthew 22:37-40 NIV)

In answering the Pharisee's question, Jesus revealed to us the real foundation on which we can stand. It is the first and greatest commandment, which means there is no greater purpose, no greater pursuit, and nothing more important. If we love Him above all else, we can endure anything—even cancer.

"My son, do not forget My teaching, but keep My commands in your heart, for they will prolong your life many years and bring you peace and prosperity." (Proverbs 3:1-2 NIV)

This battle has been such a blessing because it has shown me the power of His love for me, and it has increased my love for Him. He has provided for me in so many ways, given me such great resources to turn to on which to rely, including incredible doctors and nurses. He has been so gracious to me, even at my weakest point. He never left me alone, and I love Him all the more for it.

I don't have to have all the answers. I don't have to figure it all out. I just have to love Him and trust Him. For that reason, I pray daily for the strength to fully surrender to God.

"But God demonstrates His own love toward us, in that while we were still sinners, Christ died for us." (Romans 5:8 NIV)

In loving Him, He allows me to truly love.

In fearing Him alone, I have nothing else to fear.

In trusting Him, I can never be shaken.

In obeying Him, my path is clear.

I desire to love Him with all my heart, soul, mind, and strength, knowing that I will receive the greatest reward of all in the end: heaven.

If you only remember one command from God, let it be this: "Love the Lord your God with all your heart and with all your soul and with all your mind." Get this one right, and everything else will fall into place.

God's Plan vs. My Free Will

Monday, the PROVENGE treatment continued. They put the "supercharged" blood back in my body. Friday, I will go to Tulsa to have more blood taken out to be supercharged. Carla will have her stitches removed on Wednesday, and she starts therapy next Tuesday. I can't wait until she is healthy again. Even with this supercharged blood, I can't fill in for her in everything that she does. I just don't have the energy.

Friends have blessed us with so much support. They've brought meals to our house. They've sent encouraging messages. I see God's love in them.

I know God's plan for my life. His plan is to love me always, no matter what happens, no matter how sick I am, no matter how much I struggle. His plan is to always be there for me, standing firm in my worst moments. Even when I can't see Him, even when I forget Him in a difficult moment, His plan is to make all of His resources available to me. I can always turn to Him, because he promised to never leave me.

"God has said, 'Never will I leave you; never will I forsake you.'" (Hebrews 13:5b NIV)

God has promised that His love and resources will always be there for us. He has given each of us the ability to turn to Him, but it's a choice that we each must make. On your hardest days, do you choose to trust Him or do you turn away from Him? Do you choose to love Him and rely on His resources, or do you simply shout, "Why me? Life is so unfair!" Do you choose to follow His way or go your own way?

I have made many mistakes in my life. I have made the wrong choice many times, and I've had to learn some hard lessons as a result. Thank God for His unfailing love and forgiveness. Even with all of my bad choices, He still loves me.

The minute I heard the words, "You have cancer," I had to make my choice. When I was laid off from work ten years ago, I had to make a choice. When I lost my father years ago, I had to make a choice. In each instance, I had to decide to either trust God or give in to despair and shout, "Life is unfair!"

We are all faced with this choice many times in life.

Do you accept that you are weak and sinful, desperately in need of His help, strength, and wisdom? Do you surrender to Him and obey Him?

We must take responsibility for the choices we make in our times of trouble.

"Do not be anxious about anything, but in every situation, by prayer and petition, with thanksgiving, present your requests to God." (Philippians 4:6 NIV)

Pray about *everything*. Not just healing from cancer. Not just the big things. Not just the deep valleys. Not just your biggest needs. Pray about *everything*, and worry about *nothing*. That is the choice we all face. Let me tell you from experience, how we choose to respond makes all the difference.

I pray about everything. Instead of worrying, I put it in His hands, and then I trust His will to be done, knowing that He always hears us and

He always answers. Yes, He *always* answers our prayers, in one of three ways: 1) **Yes**, 2) **Not Yet**, or 3) **I have something better in mind for you**.

Remember what Moses said to the Israelites after they'd made some bad choices:

"And now, Israel, what does the Lord your God ask of you but to fear the Lord your God, to walk in obedience to Him, to love Him, to serve the Lord your God with all your heart and with all your soul, and to observe the Lord's commands and decrees that I am giving you today for your own good?" (Deuteronomy 10:12-13 NIV)

I pray I always choose God's plan for my life, no matter what I'm going through. Sometimes, I need a little push or a reminder to make that choice, but I know He will always love me and His resources will always be available to me. With my free will, I choose to love, trust, obey, and fear the Lord. I choose to surround myself with His love and His resources. I will take everything to Him in prayer and leave nothing to fear or worry—not even cancer.

"For we walk by faith, not by sight." (2 Corinthians 5:7 ESV)

Don't Overthink Things

The battle between my faith and Satan's cancer continues. This week, I sat for three hours while all my blood traveled out of my body and cycled back in a total of 1.8 times. I must be honest; I found myself *overthinking* the procedure: "Will this really work? Is it really destroying the cancer? Is it really helping me?"

Honestly, the treatment is more complex than I can understand. The machine made strange noises, and nurses were constantly adjusting knobs and checking my vitals every twenty minutes. It's all over my head, and when I asked questions about it, their responses sounded like another language. I didn't understand half the words they used.

This makes it so easy for the worry to sneak back in and take root. The negative voices start whispering, and doubt wants to enter my mind.

I have to actively stop the worry, reject the doubt, and trust the Lord. It doesn't matter if I understand the treatment or not. God has blessed me with great resources in all these doctors and nurses, and He has entrusted me to their care. I am still in His hands!

From what I've gathered, they are filtering my blood, taking some white blood cells and plasma and sending them off to California. Then they select the best white blood cells, attach cancer-killing medicine to them, and send them back to Highlands Oncology here in Fayetteville, where they are put back inside of me to fight the cancer. That might be a gross oversimplification, but it's the best I can do.

It doesn't matter if I understand the intricacies of my treatment. I just need to stay positive, let my body rest, and pray. Worry and doubt have no use here.

The older I get, the more I tend to overthink things. That's when the negative voices try to sneak in. They want me to question, doubt, and worry. They want my thoughts to drift off on some tangent.

Nothing good comes from overthinking. I can't figure out everything. Ultimately, I just have to trust the Lord and take the next best step. Satan wants me to worry, he wants me to place blame, he wants me to get angry at God, he wants me to doubt everyone and everything. He wants me to think I'm smarter than I am. "You have to figure this out. Think, think, think. It's up to you!"

When I start down that road, I lose my peace, my faith starts to waver, and I become frustrated and angry. I won't do it. I will trust the Lord and keep moving forward.

Cancer has revealed the schemes of the devil and brought me closer to God. It has taught me to rely on God's resources. I refuse to lose that because of my "overthinking" mind.

One thing I've learned through my many trials is that it is never wise, helpful, or beneficial to question your faith. No good ever comes from it. God's love and wisdom will help us face any problem, so the best we can ever do is surrender to Him completely and trust His will.

"Truly, I say to you, whoever does not receive the kingdom of God like a child shall not enter it." (Luke 18:17 ESV)

Carla has two more weeks in her leg brace, but she's healing well. I still find myself running in circles trying to fill in for her. I love taking care of her. It leaves me with less time to overthink. In the quiet moments, I try to focus my mind on three things: faith, family, and friends.

As adults, we're so good at overcomplicating every situation. We trust our own wisdom and accomplishments. We believe we've earned the right to question God and debate with Him. Remember, He always wins in the end. His way is always the right way.

Focus on Faith

As I finish my last PROVENGE treatment, I feel truly blessed. Thank You, Lord, for Your grace in this battle.

"Be strong and courageous. Do not be afraid or terrified because of them, for the Lord your God goes with you; He will never leave you nor forsake you." (Deuteronomy 31:6 NIV)

Ironically, it is much easier to be strong and courageous when battling cancer because I am in a battle of life and death. I am constantly reminded of my need for God. Every day, I am driven to prayer because I don't know what the future holds.

I want my faith to be just as strong once I leave this valley. When the good days come, will I still turn to God every day? Will I still be aware of my need for His love, grace, and resources? Every good thing comes from Him. All glory belongs to Him.

I pray I don't forget this on my good days.

At the same time, I have to make sure that this cancer doesn't totally consume all of my thoughts and feelings. Satan puts big, ugly things in our lives in the hope that they will take all our attention. If we are too consumed by our problems, we might fail to notice all the little bites Satan is taking out of our faith in other ways.

No matter what you're going through, keep your mind and heart centered on Christ. Focus on His will and seek His wisdom.

"Do not be anxious about anything, but in every situation, by prayer and petition, with thanksgiving, present your requests to God. And the peace of God, which transcends all understanding, will guard your hearts and your minds in Christ Jesus. Finally, brothers and sisters, whatever is true, whatever is noble, whatever is right, whatever is pure, whatever is lovely, whatever is admirable—if anything is excellent or praiseworthy—think about such things. Whatever you have learned or received or heard from Me, or seen in Me—put it into practice. And the God of peace will be with you." (Philippians 4:6-9 NIV)

I spent a great weekend with three great moms: my mother came down to visit along with my niece Mallory and her daughter, little Princess Miranda, and of course, my wife, Carla, was there. The kids and I spoiled them all weekend.

Carla gets her brace off this week, and then she will start therapy. I will get my tunnel catheter removed in a few days. I can't wait! Remember, focus on faith. We need God just as much on the good days as the bad days.

By His Grace

"For it is by grace you have been saved, through faith—and this is not from yourselves, it is the gift of God." (Ephesians 2:8 NIV)

Grace, the *free* and *unmerited* favor of God, which manifests in the salvation of sinners and the bestowal of blessings, is a gift of our loving, forgiving, all-powerful God. I feel those blessings every day, even as cancer tries to steal my hope. Through every treatment, through all the ups and downs, I feel my faith getting stronger, a faith that is also a gift from God.

Nevertheless, cancer is a war, and I can only fight one battle at a time. Fortunately, God has given me an army of doctors and nurses and loved ones to fight beside me. Let me tell you, cancer is a war that no one wants. When it enters your life, it gives a new meaning to the word *fear*. No one is safe from cancer. It can enter your life in the blink of an eye. Suddenly, one day, with no warning, you find yourself in a furious fight for your life.

"Then he got into the boat and His disciples followed Him. Suddenly a furious storm came up on the lake, so that the waves swept over the boat. But Jesus was sleeping. The disciples went and woke Him saying, 'Lord, save us! We're going to drown!' He replied, 'You of little faith, why are you so afraid?' Then He got up and rebuked the winds and the waves, and it was completely calm." (Matthew 8:23-26 NIV)

Just like the disciples, I feel fear each time I face a new battle in this ongoing war. It always seems like the waves might crash over me this time, but God has not forsaken me yet. I have seen the power of prayer time and time again as my PSA numbers dropped from 1,400 to 2.55. I give all the glory to God. However, I am mindful of the fact that Satan has not given up. Every time he loses a battle, he retreats, thinks of a new and better strategy, and comes at me again.

Losing makes him furious, and the stronger we become in our faith, the bigger a trophy we become to him. We must never forget that we have a real enemy who is crafty and relentless. Even if he can't attack us in a big way, he will take small bites, eating away at our faith through little defeats and frustrations.

"I press on to take hold of that for which Christ Jesus took hold of me. Brothers and sisters, I do not consider myself yet to have taken hold of it. But one thing I do: Forgetting what is behind and straining toward what is ahead, I press on toward the goal to win the prize for which God has called me heavenward in Christ Jesus." (Philippians 3: 12b-14 NIV)

I take one day at a time, by God's grace, forgetting what is behind me and not worrying about what tomorrow may bring. Whatever happens, I know that I am saved by His grace.

Having Faith Is Easier than Not Having Faith

Having faith in God allows me to rebalance, reawaken, reimagine, re-live, repurpose, rekindle, reinvent, reclaim, redefine, recapture, rediscover, regain, and renew myself every day.

With my faith in Him, I get better every day, no matter how sick I am or how many times I fall short, because He is all-loving, all-forgiving, all-merciful, all-gracious, and all-powerful.

He is with me every step of the way, with every breath, and He knows my every thought. He knew me before I was conceived, and He knows how many breaths I will take before my time on earth is done.

Believing this—*knowing* this—makes all the difference.

Without faith, I would question everything. I would worry about everything. I would doubt everything. It would be so much easier to lose my sense of direction. My compass would start spinning out of control. My decisions would depend entirely on me. This fight with cancer would be *so much harder.*

Never forget, Satan brought sin into this world by creating doubt and temptation in the mind of Eve through a *lie.* He uses lies to shake our faith. It wasn't for nothing that Jesus called him the father of lies.

"Now the serpent was more crafty than any of the wild animals the Lord God had made. He said to the woman, 'Did God really say, 'You must not eat from any tree in the garden'?

The woman said to the serpent, 'We may eat fruit from the trees in the garden, but God did say, 'You must not eat fruit from the tree that is in the middle of the garden, and you must not touch it, or you will die.'

'You will not certainly die,' the serpent said to the woman. 'For God knows that when you eat from it your eyes will be opened, and you will be like God, knowing good and evil.'

When the woman saw that the fruit of the tree was good for food and pleasing to the eye, and also desirable for gaining wisdom, she took some and ate it. She also gave some to her husband, who was with her, and he ate it." (Genesis 3:1-6 NIV)

Here we see exactly how the devil gets Eve to begin questioning God. He uses doubt and temptation to shake her faith, and his tactic is very effective.

What we must realize is that Satan's tactics haven't changed. He is the same crafty serpent today! Only by fully acknowledging that we are weak and sinful and desperately in need of God's help at all times can we stand against him.

"I have learned to be content whatever the circumstances. I know what it is to be in need, and I know what it is to have plenty. I have learned the secret of being content in any and every situation, whether living in plenty or in want. I can do everything through Him who gives me strength." (Philippians 4:11b-13 NIV)

Our strength comes from faith in Him. As long as we hold fast to our faith, trusting the Lord in every situation, nothing can shake us, not even cancer. Lean on Him every day. Use every resource He provides. Keep your loved ones close. Be wise to Satan's schemes.

In Christ, our victory is assured.

Is It Okay to Be Me?

"We never know how long we have to live. That's the reason the Bible says, 'Prepare to meet your God.'" (Billy Graham)

I no longer take a day, or even an hour, for granted. Knowing that cancer is lurking inside of me, I am constantly aware of my own mortality, and this is another way that cancer has made me a better person.

I think frequently about the possibility of meeting God soon, and I want to be prepared to meet Him without shame. I want to face judgment day without anxiety. Knowing that I must stand before Him, I fear Him, but this fear is a healthy respect for His majesty. It's a fear that motivates me to grow in my faith and become a better me.

"For I am the LORD your God who takes hold of your right hand and says to you, 'Do not fear; I will help you.'" (Isaiah 41:13 NIV)

I try to live each day by faith, thankful for the time that He gives me. He is always with me, even during the bad days when I struggle with doubt. No matter how strong my faith is, however, I am always aware of Satan's schemes. Without God, I am weak and sinful, and I know the enemy lurks around every corner.

"Be on your guard; stand firm in the faith; be courageous; be strong." (1 Corinthians 16:13 NIV)

Because of the devil's schemes, we must stand firm in faith at all times, for he loves to attack when we are distracted. With the Lord's grace, strength, and wisdom, we can confront the worst things Satan throws at us with courage, knowing that he cannot overcome us.

Remember, we are in control of our own attitude. It is our decision whether or not we get down on our knees daily and pray for the Holy Spirit to fill our hearts.

"Create in me a clean heart, O God, and renew a right spirit within me." (Psalm 51:10 NIV)

With God's help, and the working of the Holy Spirit within me, I am able to learn more, love more, pray more, and trust more. I am able to face each day, remembering that tomorrow is always the unknown. However, even facing the unknown, I walk with confidence knowing that when my time on earth comes to an end that will be my *real beginning*. Thanks to our savior Jesus Christ, there is heaven waiting for us.

"Thanks be to God for His indescribable gift!" (2 Corinthians 9:15 NIV)

Knowing this, let us *choose* to live courageously, made stronger daily by faith, and when we fail, when we doubt, when we make mistakes, let us turn to Him for forgiveness and restoration. Ask for help every day. Ask for forgiveness. Use every resource that God makes available to you. He is always on your side! Your walk with God isn't a performance. You don't have to fake it. It's okay to be you!

"Continue steadfastly in prayer, being watchful in it with thanksgiving." (Colossians 4:2 ESV)

As for me, I am feeling great. For the first time in a long time, I have no cancer treatments planned. My doctor says my cancer is in "a great remission." All praise and glory to God! Yes, it is certainly okay to be me. In fact, I had almost forgotten what it felt like to be me. I was so consumed with cancer, with survival.

Looking back, I can see so clearly that the Lord was with me every step of the way, even when I couldn't get out of the trap of thinking constantly, "Why me? Life is so unfair!" He was always with me.

Give Faith Time!

My cancer journey began a year ago with a simple physical. When I made the appointment that day, I had no idea the detour my life was about to take—the new journey I would make through the deep valley. It was during the physical that I discovered my PSA number was *extremely high*. The doctor said my PSA was the highest he had ever seen, so I guess I'm an overachiever.

The shock brought me instantly to my knees. I felt my impending death, and I didn't know how to break the news to my family. I made the mistake of searching for information on Google, and let me tell you, I found no hope online. Every webpage was full of dire predictions about my fate. It felt like I might as well roll over and say goodbye right then and there. Even so, I had no idea what the journey ahead of me would be like. I couldn't yet comprehend just how deep the valley was going to be.

As a result of that journey, the Lord taught me how to depend entirely on Him. He surrounded me with great doctors, loving friends and family, and He fed me with his Word. More than ever, I trust Him with every single day of my life.

"Trust in the Lord with all your heart, and do not lean on your own understanding. In all your ways acknowledge Him, and He will make straight your paths. Be not wise in your own eyes; fear the Lord, and turn away from evil. It will be healing to your flesh and refreshment to your bones." (Proverbs 3:5-8 ESV)

No matter what lies before me, I know now that He loves me, and He will be with me in every battle. Good day or bad, my faith grows stronger every day.

"When Jesus spoke again to the people, he said, 'I am the light of the world. Whoever follows me will never walk in darkness, but will have the light of life.'" (John 8:12 NIV)

When I started writing this entry, the morning sun was shining brightly, but a storm has rolled in. That's how life goes—always changing. That is why it's so important to walk in faith every moment. Always be ready, strong in the Lord, because you never know when the next storm is going to roll in.

I know that if I sit still and listen carefully by faith, I will still hear the birds singing, I will still sense the sun shining, even when the worst storm rolls into my life. His light is always shining, and Jesus is able to calm any storm. The clouds will eventually pass, but His love will never fail.

No matter how dark the clouds are today, trust the Lord. Hang onto faith, be patient, and listen to Him. He is right there beside you!

Grace Is Stronger Than "It"

God is good all the time.

His love, His grace, His wisdom, and His resources are always there for me, and I know He will never fail me, run out on me, or abandon me. His grace runs far deeper than my deepest sin, my greatest weakness, or the cancer that lies dormant in my body.

"If we are faithless, He remains faithful, for He cannot disown Himself." (2 Timothy 2:13 NIV)

No matter what I'm going through, no matter the "it" that is currently testing me, I choose to trust Him, I choose to surrender to Him, and I commit myself to obeying Him. He has blessed me so much with my faith, friends, and family—I have no excuse for focusing on the negative.

I feel great today, even though I am well aware that my "it" is still inside of me. Cancer is in remission, but that doesn't mean it's gone. Instead of letting that trouble me, I focus on the good that has happened. For example, my PSA number fell again today. It was stuck at 2.55, but it is now down to 1.91. I remind myself continually that I began this journey at 1,400.

"Do not be afraid, for I have ransomed you. I have called you by name; you are mine. When you go through deep waters, I will be with you. When you go through rivers of difficulty, you will not drown." (Isaiah 43:1b-2 NLT)

I will never have all the answers. I will never know with certainty what tomorrow holds. However, my trust and faith are in a God who does. For that, I am blessed in every situation.

"Do not be anxious about anything, but in every situation, by prayer and petition, with thanksgiving, present your requests to God. And the peace of God, which transcends all understanding, will guard your hearts and your minds in Christ Jesus." (Philippians 4:6-7 NIV)

It is my responsibility to go to God with my anxieties, my worries, and my fears. He promises to give me peace if I will do so. That is His promise for each of us. Instead of holding onto your fears, turn everything over to Him. No matter what your biggest "it" is, entrust yourself fully to God, and He will release you from the power of those fears in your life.

If you're not prepared, if you haven't laid a solid foundation in your life, it's going to be much harder to fully trust God when trouble arrives.

That's why Jesus tells us, "Therefore everyone who hears these words of mine and puts them into practice is like a wise man who built his house on the rock. The rain came down, the streams rose, and the winds blew and beat against that house; yet it did not fall, because it had its foundation on the rock." (Matthew 7:23-25 NIV)

Don't wait until you receive the worst news of your life to start building the foundation of your life upon the Rock. Jesus Himself *is* that foundation, and the resources He provides us are the blocks in that foundation.

Stand on that foundation *now* before the time of trouble so that when your next "it" arrives, you will keep standing.

Faith Is the Fuel That Keeps Me Going

Faith is the fuel of a victorious life, and unlike other kinds of fuel, it is renewable, works in every situation, is suitable for every person, and the more you share it, the more of it you have. The source of this fuel is the Lord, who is all-powerful, all-knowing, and *always* available to us at all times.

It has been a year since my first chemo treatment. This week I received the third injection of a time-released drug to fight the cancer in my body. I am very thankful I only have to get an injection every six months.

Through this long fight, my faith has kept me going. It keeps the negative voices at bay, gives me strength when my body is weak, and protects me from the side effects.

"You, dear children, are from God and have overcome them because the One who is in you is greater than the one who is in the world." (1 John 4:4 NIV)

At the doctor's appointment this week, the doctor told me he has never seen anyone go through the treatments I have and experience so few side effects. He was shocked at how my body has handled both the cancer and all the drugs I'm taking. Thank you, Lord, for your mercy. Thank you for the power of prayer.

A mind fueled by faith is a mind at peace, and a mind at peace soothes a body in need of healing.

You know the old saying, "Mind over matter?" There is some truth to it. When you put your faith at the very center of your mind, when you let it drive your thoughts, feelings, and perceptions, it has a profound effect on every area of your life. No matter what you feel in your body, you can still choose to walk by faith in Him.

By faith, take your pain and hurt and give it to Him.

By faith, give Him your sins and receive forgiveness.

By faith, turn your weakness into His strength.

The strength of our faith is the everlasting, unconditional love of the Lord. No matter how sick we might be, no matter how broken, no matter how many wrongs we have done, His love is *always* available to us.

"For I am convinced that neither death nor life, neither angels nor demons, neither the present nor the future, nor any powers, neither height nor depth, nor anything else in all creation, will be able to separate us from the love of God that is in Christ Jesus our Lord." (Romans 8:38–39 NIV)

When we walk by faith, God will take us through things we never thought we could survive, but we will *more* than survive—we will triumph. And in the end, when we walk by faith, our loving Lord will bring us to everlasting life.

"Now to Him who is able to do immeasurably more than all we ask or imagine, according to His power that is at work within us, to Him be glory in the church and in Christ Jesus throughout all generations, for ever and ever! Amen." (Ephesians 3:20-21 NIV)

What Will Your Next Step Be?

I continue to marvel at how much I have learned in this battle against cancer. I have been blessed by the Holy Spirit Who dwells in me and constantly gives me the strength I need to surrender, trust, and obey my Lord and Savior, Jesus Christ.

When I was first diagnosed with cancer, one of the doctors said, "Get your things in order."

"Get my things in order?" I replied. "What do you mean?"

"You have to understand," he said, "you do not have the normal prostate cancer. Your long-term prospects are not good."

That was fifteen months ago. I still get chills thinking about it. It was *not* a good day, to say the least, but that was the day when I started becoming a better me. Every day since then has been a blessing because I have learned to find strength in the Lord when I am weak. In my helplessness, I have learned what it means to have faith like a little child.

Nevertheless, when I first received the bad news, I had a choice to make. Don't we all? When sudden tragedy strikes, you have to decide what your next step is going to be. That next step is the most important. It will make all the difference in the days to come.

In my case, I didn't know how many steps I had left, but I decided my first step would be turning to Him in faith! Because of that, I have been so blessed throughout my battle, even when my body was at its weakest. His love and grace have carried me through some very dark days.

"God is the source of love. Christ is the proof of love. Service is the expression of love. Boldness is the outcome of love." (Henrietta Mears)

Some of my worst times turned out to be some of the biggest blessings in my life—all because my first step was to move *closer* to Him. Instead of listening to Satan's negative voices and shaking my fist at the unfairness, I chose to walk in faith, and God carried me through—and continues to carry me through.

After choosing my first step, I chose an important second step: to open myself up to friends and family, sharing my struggles with them. I could have withdrawn, feeling sorry for myself, but I didn't. I let loved ones help me carry this cross, as I tried to help them carry their own crosses. As a result, I learned how much stronger we all are together.

Together, my friends and I have grown closer, my family and I have grown in our love for each other, and all of us have become stronger in faith.

"Be devoted to one another in love. Honor one another above yourselves." (Romans 12:10)

My friends, family, and I have shed many tears together, and we have surrounded each other with prayers. Together, we are learning how to take one day at a time, trusting the Lord for our strength in every situation.

Let your friends and family be a blessing in your time of need, and be a blessing to them in return. It will make a huge difference. So many times, I *felt* their prayers. I really did *feel* them.

What a blessing!

"As iron sharpens iron so one person sharpens another." (Proverbs 27:17)

Put the First Thing First Always!

I am feeling great these days, and it's my favorite time of year once again: football season! It's great to feel like the old Dan again, but at the same time, something is very different now. I couldn't put my finger on what it is that is so different about me, but then it hit me: I have never felt closer to the Lord than I do right now.

Wow, did Satan's plan completely backfire or what? He hit me with his best shot; but instead of losing my faith, I am standing stronger than ever before. Choosing to trust the Lord when my world fell apart made all the difference.

Because of my desperation, I turned to the Lord daily. I surrounded myself with loved ones, and I felt the power of prayer. Despite the weakness in my body, I have never felt such power in my life. Even as my body wasted away, I was winning the spiritual battle day by day.

Now that I feel so much better, I have to be careful. When you're walking through a deep, dark valley, you *feel* Him. You find yourself crying out to Him because you have nowhere else to turn.

Once you come out of the valley, it becomes so easy to forget that you need the Lord just as much now as you did then. I don't want to lose sight of the powerful lessons I learned on my worst days:

1. When my body was weakest, I became strong.
2. When I was on the verge of losing hope, the Lord surrounded me with all the resources I needed.
3. I can feel the power and presence of the prayers my friends and family offer up on my behalf. We are truly stronger together in Him.
4. God never, ever leaves us.

I want to remember all of this on my good days.

"I am with you always." (Matthew 28:20 ESV)

Will I lose everything I gained just because I am doing so well now? No, I refuse!

"Therefore, since we are surrounded by such a great cloud of witnesses, let us throw off everything that hinders and the sin that so easily entangles. And let us run with perseverance the race marked out for us, fixing our eyes on Jesus, the Pioneer and Perfecter of faith. For the joy set before Him, he endured the cross, scorning its shame, and sat down at the right hand of the throne of God. Consider Him who endured such opposition from sinners, so that you will not grow weary and lose heart." (Hebrews 12:1-3 NIV)

Remember, no matter how good today might be, the enemy can attack at any time. Things can change in a moment. Life will never be fair. Therefore, even on my best days, I will surround myself with my faith, family, and friends, knowing we are stronger together in Him.

The very next step in my journey could be another descent into a valley of sin, sickness, hurt, or loss. Although I will not walk in fear, I will stay mindful of Satan's tactics. He wants my eyes fixed on anything but Jesus.

During these good days, when I'm starting to feel like my old self, I will remember to maintain my focus on the one and only thing that really matters: the love of God. I give Him the glory for these good days, but I know that He will prepare me if trouble should arise again.

When you're doing well, it's so easy to get distracted by the things of this world. For this reason, in both the good and bad days, we must remember this:

"Finally, brothers and sisters, whatever is true, whatever is noble, whatever is right, whatever is pure, whatever is lovely, whatever is admirable—if anything is excellent or praiseworthy—think about such things." (Philippians 4:8 NIV)

Thankful for the Storms

Terrible storms have hit Texas and Florida recently, and so many lives have been changed forever as a result. So many have lost everything, including loved ones. At the same time, in the aftermath of the storms, we've seen communities coming together to help one another. Neighbors are helping neighbors.

Yes, storms bring people together, and that togetherness is a reason to feel grateful, even in the midst of our suffering. There is never a good time for a storm, but they are going to come. What matters is how we choose to handle them. Do we support one another? Do we see others going through storms and reach out to them? Do we open up to others when we are going through our own storms?

Texas and Florida will rebuild. They will bounce back stronger, not just structurally but spiritually. We are covering them in prayer and sharing with them generously.

Should we be thankful for the storms that hit us? It might not make sense, but I am grateful for the life-threatening sickness that came into my life. It made me a better person. My love for the Lord is stronger than ever. I am closer to my friends and family. Believe it or not, even though I don't want to be sick, I wouldn't trade it for anything.

"Therefore, since we have been justified through faith, we have peace with God through our Lord Jesus Christ, through Whom we have gained access by faith into this grace in which we now stand. And we boast in the hope of the glory of God. Not only so, but we also glory in our sufferings because we know that suffering produces perseverance; perseverance, character; and character, hope. And hope does not put us to shame because God's love has been poured out into our hearts through the Holy Spirit, Who has been given to us." (Romans 5:1-5 NIV)

This storm of cancer helped me understand what is truly important in life. Yes, as incredible as it sounds, cancer turned out to be a tremendous blessing. I see now that there are some things we just can't learn until the storms hit. Furthermore, I know that if and when another storm sweeps into my life, I will be able to persevere. In fact, when I see the next storm coming, I'm ready to hit it head on, fully trusting in the Lord to get me through it.

Let the Lord show you His power, His strength, His love, His goodness when the storms hit. Let him bring you closer to your friends and family. Let Him teach you and guide you day by day.

Yes, let the storms of life be a blessing!

Blessings Come from Our Worst Times

When bad times hit, we have to pause and think carefully about how we're going to respond. Our initial response will set us on a course that will make a big difference in our lives as the journey unfolds.

I experienced one of my worst times almost ten years ago: the day I lost my job. I worked at Sam's Club, and I loved it. I was successful at my job, and I fully expected—and intended—to stay there until retirement. And then one day, out of the blue, I was laid off. The parent company, Walmart, decided to massively downsize, and I was one of many who found themselves out of a job. Suddenly, my future career plans were all gone, completely gone.

It hit me hard, and I wasn't prepared for it. Neither were my coworkers. Many of them were shocked. How could this have happened?

I remember leaving work that day, and my mind was reeling. What was I supposed to do now? What was my next step going to be? Who was I without that name badge pinned to my shirt? Was I even the same person anymore?

Layoffs are a part of life, unfortunately, but if you've been through one, you know it's never easy. Not only does it threaten your financial stability, but suddenly there are so many decisions to make about your future. All of your long-term plans go right out the window.

During that time, I received a lot of advice from friends and family. Some of it was good, and some of it was not so good. Ultimately, I chose to press pause on my life and take a step back.

It's in these moments when Satan likes to sneak in and start whispering. He wants us to fall into despair. He wants us to blame God and get angry. He wants us to start the endless litany of complaints. If I had given in and gone down the path of blame and bitterness, I might have missed out on what God had in mind.

You see, ironically, one of the best things that ever happened to me came about as a direct result of that layoff. As I struggled to pick up the pieces of my shattered career, I was invited by a friend to attend a weekly men's group.

That men's group has turned out to be one of the most important resources in my life. It's a place where guys support and encourage each other, a place where it's okay to be weak and admit that you're a sinner. It's a group devoted to being in fellowship, gaining strength from one another, and praying for one another.

That men's group has been absolutely vital during my battle with cancer. Isn't it interesting how one of my worst experiences led me to a resource that helped me get through another one of my worst experiences? God works that way.

That experience ten years ago was horrible for me and for my whole family, and I can remember it all very clearly. It seems like it was yesterday. To this day, I still thank God for leading me through that difficult time. More than that, I thank Him for transforming one of my worst experiences into one of my greatest blessings.

God has a purpose in everything. It's not always easy to see it, but we can choose to trust Him anyway. I would never have guessed ten years ago that God was preparing me to fight cancer.

Trust God in everything. Let the Holy Spirit fill you and give you peace in every circumstance. God has a greater purpose, and someday you will see it.

Satan's Playbook

It has been a year since my last chemo treatment. Recently, I looked at a picture of myself during that time, and I couldn't believe how bad I looked—even worse than I felt, and that's saying something because I felt awful. Suffice it to say, God gave me hair for a reason.

It really shows the brutality of our enemy. Remember, he comes only to steal, kill, and destroy. We do well not to forget that Satan is a tough opponent who plays by no rules. He is deceptive, he is conniving, and he is clever. He's also persistent, and his goal is to create doubt and worry. In his rebellion against God, he will use anyone he can, and he is underhanded.

Satan has nothing to lose because he already knows he has lost. He knows that God is going to win in the end, but he's determined to go down swinging, taking as many souls with him as he can.

Thankfully, because I belong to Christ, I know where I will be going in the end. The Lord has already promised my destination.

"The Lord will fulfill His purpose for me; Your steadfast love, O Lord, endures forever." (Psalm 138:8a ESV)

Only the Lord knows when I will reach that destination. He has already appointed my time. Therefore, I choose to live my life as if each day could be my last. That doesn't mean I'm going to pick up skydiving or bull riding. It just means I intend to live my life to the fullest, walking in faith, enjoying my time with friends and family—each and every day.

However, I also intend to stay alert, knowing that the enemy is still at work. For that reason, because Satan is crafty and persistent, we all need to have a game plan for life. Don't just stumble along and give him the opportunity to sneak up on you!

To defend against an enemy, you have to understand his playbook. I want to become familiar with all of Satan's little trick plays so I can always mount an effective defense. I intend to be ready at all times in this battle. The enemy is out there. I can't afford to become complacent.

The best defense we have is a good offense, which is why it's so important to maintain your prayer life, stay in close fellowship with friends and family, and nourish yourself with God's Word. Put on the full armor of God and *keep it on*. Don't take any pieces of armor off just because you're having a good day.

"Therefore, put on the full armor of God, so that when the day of evil comes, you may be able to stand your ground, and after you have done everything, to stand. Stand firm then, with the belt of truth buckled around your waist, with the breastplate of righteousness in place, and with your feet fitted with the readiness that comes from the gospel of peace. In addition to all this, take up the shield of faith, with which you can extinguish all the flaming arrows of the evil one. Take the helmet of salvation and the sword of the Spirit, which is the word of God." (Ephesians 6:13-17 NIV)

You also need allies in the battle because the people who fight beside you are going to make a big difference in the outcome. Do you have fellowship with people who build you up in faith? Do they encourage you and pray for and with you? Do they help carry your burdens, as you help carry theirs? A bad friend in a time of need can become a voice of

Satan, feeding you doubt, fear, and anger. They will get you to play the blame game.

"Don't befriend angry people or associate with hot-tempered people, or you will learn to be like them and endanger your soul." (Proverbs 22:24-25 NLT)

Also, remember that you win the war by winning the small battles. There are times when I don't even realize I'm being attacked. Satan is good at whispering so quietly that he inserts himself into my thoughts before I even know he's doing it. This is one of his sneakiest moves.

Suddenly, I find myself doing or saying something I shouldn't, driven by fear, anger, or sin, and I have a spectacular fall. Embarrassed, I get back up, shake it off, and say, "Why didn't I see that coming? How many times am I going to let this happen?"

This is why it's so important to be mindful of Satan's tricks. Don't let him weaken your faith in any area of your life, no matter how small.

Remember the old parable about boiling a frog? It goes something like this: How do you boil a frog without it jumping out of the pot? You put it in a pot of cool water. The frog won't jump out because it feels good. Then you slowly—so slowly that the frog doesn't notice—turn up the heat. Before the frog realizes it's in danger, the water is boiling, and the frog is cooked.

Satan does the same thing with his little tricks. He weakens our faith not by taking one big bite out of our armor but by nibbling along the edges. Often, we don't even realize he's doing it until one day, in the midst of some spiritual battle, we find ourselves defenseless.

I believe the devil has won more souls through these small, unnoticed attacks than anything else. When the devil tried a big play on me—cancer—it backfired. He made my faith stronger than ever. The shock sent me fleeing to God. Satan took his best shot, and God and I are winning.

Just this week, my PSA hit a new low of 0.9. All glory to God. Yes, Satan, you are losing.

It's in the little fights that I have to be careful. I expect Satan to come against me with some life-changing attack, but I don't always see the little things: temptations, frustrations, disappointments, and so on. Fortunately, I know his game plan, and I have a Head Coach who is able to counter any offensive maneuver. I just have to keep my eyes open.

Be mindful of the small bites! Walk in the Holy Spirit every day, even if everything is going your way at the moment. Surrender, trust, and obey the Lord on the good days. Don't become complacent. Don't let the enemy have even the smallest victories in your life. Trust our Head Coach, stick close to the right teammates, and the Lord, whose game plan is perfect, will keep you strong in the faith.

The best play of all is God's love for us.

"God is love." (1 John 4:16 NIV)

Make the Most of the Greatest Gift Ever

The Christmas season is upon us once again. It's so much easier during this time of year to focus on the greatest gift rather than the cancer that is still in my body. I want to remember this lesson throughout the year: focus on the blessings, not the problems.

"For God so loved the world that He gave His one and only Son, that whoever believes in Him shall not perish but have eternal life." (John 3:16 NIV)

Jesus is the greatest gift God ever gave us. God's one and only Son was born, lived a perfect life, and taught us His Father's ways. He died a terrible death on the cross to atone for our sins, and then He conquered death by rising again on the third day. In doing so, He reconciled us to the Father, and God sent the Holy Spirit to be with us, dwelling in our souls, hearts, and minds every step we take on the earth.

We are very blessed because of Christmas and Easter. These seasons give us the perfect opportunity to re-orient our lives in Christ because they naturally draw our minds and hearts to the joy we have in Him.

"I am the gate; whoever enters through Me will be saved. They will come in and go out, and find pasture." (John 10:9 NIV)

All the clichés are true: Jesus is the reason for the season, and He is the gift that keeps on giving. This gift is "one size fits all," never wears out, never breaks, and even if you return it, He will still be available to you. Are we making the most of this amazing gift? Remember, this encouragement from Scripture:

"Therefore, since we are surrounded by such a great cloud of witnesses, let us throw off everything that hinders and the sin that so easily entangles. And let us run with perseverance the race marked out for us, fixing our eyes on Jesus, the Pioneer and Perfecter of faith. For the joy set before Him He endured the cross, scorning its shame, and sat down at the right hand of the throne of God." (Hebrews 12:1-2 NIV)

Jesus is a gift who is meant to be shared with everyone, in word and deed. We share Him when we love, listen, encourage, learn, cry, and pray together in faith and hope. In doing so, we become stronger together. Be grateful for the greatest gift of all. Share this gift with everyone around you.

Lord, make me an instrument of your peace

Where there is hatred, let me sow love

Where there is injury, pardon

Where there is doubt, faith

Where there is despair, hope

Where there is darkness, light

And where there is sadness, joy

O Divine Master, grant that I may

Not so much seek to be consoled as to console

To be understood, as to understand

To be loved, as to love

For it is in giving that we receive

And it's in pardoning that we are pardoned

And it's in dying that we are born to Eternal Life.

(attributed to St. Francis of Assisi)

Tomorrow Has Not Been Promised

New Year's Day is upon us. As we enter a new year, we think about what the future holds. People make plans, they make resolutions, they hope for better days. However, we can be so focused on our future hopes and dreams that we forget that the *future is not guaranteed.*

"As it was in the days of Noah, so it will be at the coming of the Son of Man. For in the days before the flood, people were eating and drinking, marrying and giving in marriage, up to the day Noah entered the ark; and they knew nothing about what would happen until the flood came and took them all away. That is how it will be at the coming of the Son of Man." (Matthew 24: 37-39 NLT)

We have today, we have *right now,* but the clock is ticking. At an appointed hour, the Lord will return and that will be the end of all those earthly plans. If you're not right with the Lord, don't put it off any longer. Tomorrow has not been promised to any of us.

When I was battling cancer, I had no idea if I would live to see the next year. I was thankful for every day because I didn't know how much longer I had.

Cancer is dormant within me now, and things are going much better, but the reality of tomorrow hasn't changed. None of us knows how much time we have left on earth. Only God knows the number of our days. Instead of letting this drive us to despair and fear, we should live in readiness.

Even if we don't have something like cancer to serve as a stark reminder, we all face battles daily as we strive to walk with the Lord. Doubt, despair, worry, anger, and temptations are thrown our way each day. The enemy wants nothing more than to destroy our faith, and he is relentless. Every day, we experience small victories and small defeats. The war rages on! Never forget.

Instead of putting your hope in the upcoming year, in a tomorrow that you are not guaranteed, take one day at a time. Focus on *being* in relationship with God today—right now—and leave all of the tomorrows in His hands.

Though the war rages on, we are never alone. In sickness, hurt, and loss, God is with us. In the unfairness of life, God's love is never far from us. Love always wins because He *is* love. No hurt or sin is greater than His love for you.

"The LORD is compassionate and gracious, slow to anger, abounding in love." (Psalm 103:8 NIV)

Therefore, by the grace of God, focus on today. Walk closely with Him, and always remember that He has a purpose for whatever you're going through right now.

"And we know that in all things God works for the good of those who love Him, who have been called according to His purpose." (Romans 8:28 NIV)

I have no idea what this new year holds for me, but my goal is to be ever-prepared for anything, good or bad. Daily, I will surrender, trust, and obey the Lord, so that no matter what comes my way, I will stand strong. God knows my appointed time, and that is enough for me.

Light Battling Darkness

"You have to expect spiritual warfare whenever you stand up for right-eousness or call attention to basic values. It's just a matter of light battling the darkness. But the light wins every time. You can't throw enough darkness on light to put it out." (Thomas Kinkade)

I try to walk in the light of Christ at all times, but to be honest, there are times when I still feel the darkness trying to creep in. After all, the cancer is still in me, and the devil is still up to all of his old schemes. If I'm not careful, I could quickly become overwhelmed.

In the darkness, we feel only fear and confusion. Because of the uncertainty, every step can feel like an eternity. It becomes so much easier to give in to anger, hate, despair. Sadly, there is a lot of darkness in the world around us.

Thankfully, the light of Christ is brighter than any darkness, and that light is within us, which means we *never* have to walk in darkness. No matter what evil we're dealing with, no matter how severe the trial, we can always choose to stand in God's light by believing, trusting, and obeying Him.

I have seen that light shining in pitch-black darkness, when my whole body felt like it had wasted away to nothing, when despair and fear were coming at me from every direction. Never forget, when you shine with the light of Christ in a dark place, you become a much bigger and more obvious target for Satan.

As the light shines brighter and brighter, expect the enemy to come against you. Spiritual warfare is inevitable. The only hope Satan has in his kingdom of darkness is to diminish your light by covering it with sin. He can never snuff out the light of Christ completely—our Lord is simply too bright—but he can certainly make it appear dimmer.

Satan's victory is only ever temporary. We know who wins in the end. The light of Christ is destined to shine forever and ever, so let that light continue to shine in your life. Never allow the enemy to put anything in the way to diminish it.

"Let your light shine before men, that they may see your good deeds and praise your Father in heaven." (Matthew 5:16 NLT)

But how do we make the light of Christ shine more brightly, even in the darkness? By continuing to trust Him, no matter what happens. By continuing to follow Him, even when the enemy throws every trick in the book at us. By continuing to reveal Him in the ways we act, speak, and live.

Stay close to family and friends, especially those who desire to walk in the light. Be a mutual encouragement to one another. We walk best when we walk in the light together.

"I love those who love me, and those who seek me find me." (Proverbs 8:17 NIV)

The more we seek the Lord and the more we love Him, the brighter His love and grace will shine in our lives. Then our fear of the darkness will fade away as He fills every corner of our lives.

"There is no fear in love. But perfect love drives out fear, because fear has to do with punishment. The one who fears is not made perfect in love." (1 John 4:18 NIV)

Surrender, trust, and obey the Lord in whatever you're going through right now. He has enabled you to make that choice. It doesn't matter how dark it seems. Surrender, trust, and obey Him.

"Your word is a lamp to my feet and a light to my path." (Psalm 119:105 ESV)

The Importance of Being Fun-Loving

One of the things I've learned in my long battle with cancer is that you must find ways to have fun along the way. It's good for the soul. Fun doesn't come easy during times of trouble, but I can tell you that some of my most special times in the last few years came from laughing and having fun with friends and family. Fun does wonders for a mind and body in pain.

Even in pain, there is still *fun* in faith, *fun* in fellowship, *fun* in worship, *fun* in praise, and *fun* in prayer because all of these can bring us great joy.

"The Lord is my strength and my shield; my heart trusts in Him, and He helps me. My heart leaps for joy, and with my song I praise Him." (Psalm 28:7 NIV)

The days are so evil. Make sure to carve out a little time for having fun. It is so important, and so good for us. The battle is deadly serious, so sometimes I have to actively remind myself to laugh and enjoy myself. No matter what I'm going through, I *need* those joyful times. We all do.

I will never take the time I have with friends and family for granted ever again. They've meant so much to me, and made such a difference in my battles, that I want them by my side every day. We need joyful times together, fun times. We need to enjoy each other's company and fellowship in the Lord. When I look back at my worst days, I realize just how important those fun times with friends and family were to me, how they got me through and kept me going.

"Life really must have joy. It's supposed to be fun!" (Barbara Bush, Commencement Address to Wellesley College Class of 1990)

My father set a great example for me in this regard. He lost his mother when he was only fifteen, but he was blessed with friends, family, and a supportive small-town community. Then he married my mom, and the two of them always managed to have fun, no matter how little they had. To this day we still laugh about some of my baby pictures, which have "proof" stamped right in the middle of them.

We were a family of four, and my parents always worked hard. It wasn't easy, but we had fun. At one time, we lost our home due to a business deal that didn't work out, and my father had to file for bankruptcy. After that, we moved from our home into a basement apartment. It was a big adjustment, and it didn't come easy. By that point, my sister was married and had a new baby. We'd lost our house, but the new addition to our family was such a blessing.

The bankruptcy could have been devastating, but because of the way my parents handled it, we were okay. Yes, we struggled, but my parents made sure that we were still a fun-loving family. They made time for fun, and they continued to rejoice in what we had: faith, family, and friends. I am so thankful for their example.

Later, when I worked for Walmart, I felt tremendously blessed to work for such a great company founded by one of the greatest business leaders of all time, Sam Walton, a man who knew the importance of having fun during stressful times. He always found ways to inject a little entertainment into the business. Famously, this led to his celebrating the company's success by performing a hula dance on Wall Street in 1984. You can find videos of the incident online. What a great lesson, not only in business but in life.

But how in the world can you have fun when you have cancer? I remember one example. After my last chemo treatment, I thought the worst was over. I was finished, moving on, and the old Dan was back. Let's go! Little did I know I was about to experience one of the biggest setbacks in my entire cancer journey.

My absolute lowest point occurred after that last chemo treatment. What I didn't realize is that all of the chemo was building up inside of me. Eventually, the cumulative effect hit me all at once, and I crumbled. Every single part of my body hurt. My fingers and toes hurt. My bones hurt. I was swelled up like a dead pig. All of my hair was gone. I didn't think it was possible to feel so awful.

So what did I do?

I made a cup of coffee and went to the hot tub. My older daughter had left her sunglasses on the rim of the hot tub the day before. It was early, so I was the only one awake in the house. As I got in the water, I was feeling sorry for myself, and then I did it. I reached over, picked up my daughter's sunglasses, put them on, and took a selfie. There I was—big, fat, and bald, wearing a pair of girlish sunglasses, with steam coming off the top of my head. It was ridiculous, so, of course, I sent the picture to the family, waking them all up. They started that day with a laugh after they got over my waking them up so early.

The laughter didn't make the pain go away, but it did change my attitude. Sharing that amusing little moment with loved ones helped me face the day just a bit more easily. It actually made the pain more bearable.

Don't get so caught up in the pain that you forget to laugh. If someone else is in pain, help him or her remember how to smile again. Have fun in your faith. There's power in it.

Fear Is a Liar! Be Free!

My battle with Satan's cancer forced me to face death head on. As a result, I no longer feel any fear of death. I know now that our true prize is not of this world.

"I am prepared to die. In fact, I'm looking forward to it. And when you're prepared to die, you're also prepared to live." (Billy Graham)

I have said that cancer made me a better person, brought me close to the Lord, and taught me many important lessons. One of those lessons is the realization that I can live in freedom from fear. Cancer is still inside my body, but I can live with cancer and not be afraid. What freedom!

Jesus is my rock. I stand firm no matter what. He has delivered me from the fear of death!

"Be strong and courageous. Do not fear or be in dread of them, for it is the Lord your God who goes with you. He will not leave you or forsake you." (Deuteronomy 31:6 ESV)

In learning to overcome fear, I discovered that I am sometimes my own worst enemy. First, I start to feel anxiety. Then I allow it to take root and become worried. I let the worry build until it becomes fear, and before I know it, I'm in a terrible state of mind.

Fear lies to us. We must make the choice not to listen to it. Fear will fill you with despair, if you let it. "God has abandoned you. Cancer wins, and you lose. You are not loved. You're just a weak, sinful man. Why would God care about you?"

Yes, we are all weak and sinful. Yes, we are all going to die someday. But we are loved. We are very loved, and God never abandons us. He walks with us every step of the way, and He will help us in our weakness if we lean on Him. I must remember daily to reject the lies. I have to fill my heart, my soul, and my life with the Holy Spirit and walk in freedom!

"The Spirit gives life; the flesh counts for nothing. The words I have spoken to you—they are full of the Spirit and life." (John 6:63 NIV)

Through the Holy Spirit, we feel God's love, and God's love delivers us from fear. But we must use all of God's resources to keep it from taking root. The power of prayer, the support of friends and family, and the Word of God are weapons against this tool of Satan.

Trust God. Walk in freedom. Don't listen to fear!

Making Promises

My PSA has gone from its peak of 1,400 to a new low of 0.7. I promise this: I will never forget how strong I was when I was at my absolute weakest. I will never forget how *real* God's love for me was when I hit the lowest point. I will never forget the importance of sharing my struggles, my ugliness, and my pain with friends and asking for their prayers and guidance.

I will never forget all I have learned from this long battle. I promise I will continue to use all of God's resources in my life. On the bad days and good days, I will listen, follow, and praise him. I will not fear the things of this world; I will only fear the Lord.

Can you make these promises as well?

"Listen to counsel and accept discipline, that you may be wise the rest of your days." (Proverbs 19:20 NASB)

"The fear of the LORD is the beginning of knowledge; fools despise wisdom and instruction." (Proverbs 1:7 NIV)

Fear of the Lord is not something terrible. We fear Him so that we may be free from all other fears. We fear Him because He is all-knowing. He knows every thought we have, every word we say, every move we make, and there is no hiding from Him.

Yes, we are fully known, but we are also loved.

For that reason, I promise to trust Him, no matter what my future holds. I promise to remember the hard lessons. I promise to go to Him in prayer rather than trusting my own understanding because I've learned how important His guidance is.

"Trust in the Lord with all your heart and lean not on your own understanding; in all your ways submit to Him, and He will make your paths straight. Do not be wise in your own eyes; fear the Lord and shun evil. This will bring health to your body and nourishment to your bones." (Proverbs 3:5-8 NIV)

I promise I will flee from evil and run to the Lord. I will turn all of my worries, fears, and sins over to Him. I will ask for forgiveness. I will pray for others. I will ask the Holy Spirit to fill my heart, mind, and soul, so that I can surrender, trust, and obey the Lord in everything.

Can you make these promises with me?

"He fulfills the desires of those who fear Him; He hears their cry and saves them." (Psalm 145:19 NIV)

Satan's Cancer Will Not Define Me

When you're battling cancer, it can consume all of your time and all of your thoughts if you're not careful. When that happens, you can get so caught up in the *problem* that you forget to focus on what matters most.

As soon as the doctor told me I had stage IV cancer, as soon as he said those fateful words, "Get your things in order," I began to wage a very unproductive war in my mind. I began to struggle with anger, with "why me," with sleepless nights full of worry, with despair over all of the things I was going to miss.

I was consumed with all of the negative things. I experienced first-hand how easy it was to let the darkness control me. Fear, anger, and self-pity spread in my mind like wildfire. It can do the same in yours if you're not careful, and that's exactly what Satan wants.

One of the reasons I keep calling this "Satan's cancer" is because I saw how he wanted to use it as a tool for intensifying all the negative within me. It was like pouring gasoline on a fire. He wanted me to become so filled with negative emotions that I would be utterly useless for the kingdom.

Anyone can find a reason to stay angry. Anyone can find a reason to complain about the unfairness of life. We must resist the urge. If we let these negative thoughts take over, we are essentially handing control of our lives over to Satan.

This is the devil's plan. This is what he does. This is how he operates. It's why the world is filled with sin and cruelty. It's why so many people are blaming others, fighting others, hurting others. It's why so many people are angry all the time.

"But mark this: There will be terrible times in the last days. People will be lovers of themselves, lovers of money, boastful, proud, abusive, disobedient to their parents, ungrateful, unholy, without love, unforgiving, slanderous, without self-control, brutal, not lovers of the good, treacherous, rash, conceited, lovers of pleasure rather than lovers of God—having a form of godliness but denying its power. Have nothing to do with such people." (2 Timothy 3:1-5 NIV)

This Scripture passage hit me hard today as I thought about all of the victories Satan seems to be having in the lives of people around the world. He has so many people completely wrapped up in their negative thoughts. The war rages all around us, and it's a war that is so much more important than battling cancer.

The battle between good and evil, light and darkness, is the *real* battle, and we are all pawns in the fight.

"Devote yourselves to prayer, being watchful and thankful." (Colossians 4:2 NIV)

I have learned to be watchful and mindful any time Satan tries to stir up anger inside of me. I will not fall for his schemes. He tries to divide people. He wants us at each other's throats.

When I sense him trying to do this in my life now, I stop whatever I'm doing and go straight to prayer, handing whatever is bothering me over to the Lord. When I find myself in a struggle, I seek the support and encouragement of family and friends. I will not allow Satan to have a foothold in my mind or in my heart.

"Follow God's example, therefore, as dearly loved children and walk in the way of love, just as Christ loved us and gave Himself up for us as a fragrant offering and sacrifice to God." (Ephesians 5:1-2 NIV)

I want my life to be defined by my love, faith, and trust in the Lord, no matter what Satan throws my way. For that reason, I ask the Lord daily to fill my heart, mind, and soul with the Holy Spirit, so I can be a reflection of Christ and His ways.

"By this everyone will know that you are my disciples, if you love one another." (John 13:35 NIV)

Yes, we're in the midst of a war for our souls, but I know who wins in the end. Satan will go down fighting, but he will go down. He wants to take as many with him as he can, so don't be a casualty of his defeat.

I will not be defined by cancer. I will not be defined by negative emotions. I will be defined by my love, faith, and trust in the Lord.

Are you with me?

The Power of Compassion

I can't believe it has been almost two years since I learned I have cancer. By the time I found out, the cancer had already been in me for a long time, as Satan planned his attack. All the doctor did was make it known to me.

It goes to show that Satan is always scheming, even when we're unaware of him. No matter how strong you think you are, no matter how good things seem to be going, he is lurking around somewhere. He loves to strike when we least expect it, and if we're not ready, he can bring us to our knees in the blink of an eye.

For that reason, I strongly encourage you not to wait until trouble strikes to strengthen your faith. Surround yourself with loving people of faith, grow in wisdom, and draw near to God right now. Right now! That way you'll be ready when Satan strikes. He won't be able to catch you off guard.

I only found out about my cancer early enough to fight it because my older daughter insisted I get a physical. Listening to a trusted loved one saved my life. I am so blessed that God put her in my life and that we were close enough for her to make the request. If not for her, I wouldn't be here today.

We are all truly stronger together in Him.

Never forget, God puts people in your life for a reason. He uses each of us as resources to help one another in times of need. Just as Satan has many schemes, our Lord has many resources to help us fight the good fight, including Scripture, the Holy Spirit, doctors, and loved ones.

The Lord uses us to strengthen one another, and I am so thankful for those who have poured out prayers on my behalf. We are all connected by the Father's love for us and by our faith in Him.

Just like a lion will single out a lone zebra from the herd, Satan looks for those who wander off by themselves. He knows that we are weaker in the faith when we are alone, isolated.

"And so we know and rely on the love God has for us. God is love. Whoever lives in love lives in God, and God in them." (1 John 4:16 NIV)

Live in the love of Christ! Live in the community of people of faith!

God intends for us to strengthen each other. You will never feel more loved than when people help carry your burdens during your time of need. There is such power in compassion! We find the Lord's favor when we pray for one another, care for one another, and encourage one another.

I would never have truly experienced this if I hadn't gone through my time in the deepest valley.

It's amazing what you learn when you're at your weakest, if you're willing. I will never forget the power of compassion. As others poured into my life, I now pour into the lives of others. I want to be a resource of God for people in their times of trouble.

I want to give more than I receive.

"Whoever brings blessing will be enriched, and one who waters will himself be watered." (Proverbs 11:25 ESV)

In My Weakness, I Am Strong

I came across this quote today, and it really hit me hard:

"Dream as if you'll live forever, live as if you'll die today."

It's attributed to James Dean, but it hit close to home. In my long fight with cancer, I've had to constantly remind myself to live. I want to live strong and finish strong in my faith, surrounded by my friends and family. The only reason any of us are able to do this is because of God's absolute love for us.

He *is* our strength, and He holds us together through good days and bad.

Honestly, I find it harder to be strong in my faith during the good days. It was so much easier when I was in the heat of battle, when chemo was ravaging my body. I was utterly weak, so I turned to Him constantly in prayer.

In my body, I am standing strong today. Even though the cancer is still present, I feel so good that I often forget I am dying. Of course, we're all dying, and we rarely know the day or hour when our life on earth will be over. That's what makes the James Dean quote so relevant. Since we don't know how much time is left, shouldn't we live every day to the fullest?

I know God is with me every day, every step, and with every breath I take, but in my strength, when I feel so good, it's easy to forget. I am not always mindful that He is with me wherever I go. My mind and heart drift.

Haven't you found that it is much easier to cry out to God continually when your whole world is falling apart? In our need, we can't help but be mindful of Him because we are desperate.

I do not want to forget Him on my good days. I have seen His power at work in the deepest valley, and I have felt His grace in the darkness. God, never let me forget. Let me always walk close to You. Help me continue to live by faith with my family and friends as I did in the heat of battle.

"Praise the LORD, O my soul; all my inmost being, praise His holy name." (Psalm 103:1 NIV)

Satan can use our good times, our prosperity, and our success against us, turning our hearts away from the Lord. Throughout my life, I have found myself falling for this scheme over and over.

We must remember that God has a purpose for both the good days as well as the bad. We need Him just as much to accomplish His will in our lives when everything seems to be going our way. We need the fellowship of friends and family just as much when we feel fantastic. He is the Lord of *all* of our days.

Let us pray that the Holy Spirit will fill our hearts and minds today, whether it's a good day or bad. Let us pray that He will enable us to surrender, trust, and obey Him today, whether we are weak or strong. Let us pray for His will to be done in our lives, whatever we're going through right now.

On good days and bad days, stay strong in the Lord who loves us. All glory belongs to Him.

Double Down on Hope

I am so thankful for great messages I receive from my pastor Ronnie Floyd. They always give me wisdom and renewed hope, no matter what I'm going through. The value of a good pastor cannot be overstated. Cross Church has been another great resource of God in my life, building my faith and strengthening my ties with friends and family. That's what a good church does for us.

Pastor Floyd's sermon today was called "Big Faith that Calls Things into Existence That Do Not Exist." Just the title alone really struck me, and it is on my mind now as I write this entry.

Satan hates our faith, and he hits us hard when he can. Well, that's okay because I know I can hit back simply by maintaining my faith and hope in God. When Satan says, "You're defeated. It's all over," faith says, "The effective prayer of a righteous man can accomplish much." (James 5:16 NIV)

Want to hit the devil back twice as hard as he's hit you? Then stand firm in your faith, trusting God, no matter what happens. Choose to trust Him, knowing that God's grace is always with you. Never forget, God is big enough for any situation, no matter how bleak Satan makes it seem.

Dare to hope in the Lord's deliverance, no matter how dark things get, praying and patiently waiting. Stack hope on top of hope. Double down on hope! When Satan's little voice whispers that you are unworthy, remind yourself of what the Scripture says:

"For it is by grace you have been saved, through faith; and this is not from yourself, it is the gift of God." (Ephesians 2:8 NIV)

When you can't see anything else, see God and hold on tight. There is nothing more discouraging to the devil than this. Events will unfold in God's time according to God's will, but His will for your life is loving and good. You must *choose* to believe this, and ask Him to help your unbelief.

"For nothing will be impossible with God." (Luke 1:37 ESV)

In this fight of mine, I have seen the power of prayer, the power of faith, the power of hope. When you're told you have stage IV cancer, when the doctors said, "You're PSA is over 1,400, and I've never seen a number that high," it is easy to think God has abandoned you and He no longer has a good will for your life.

Only through faith, through ceaseless prayer, and the prayers of friends and family, was I able to keep my eyes on God. When my body was broken, my decision to trust the Lord *no matter what* carried me through the darkness.

It has been two years since the fight began, and my PSA is currently at 0.7. All glory to God for His mercy and kindness to me. Whatever the future holds, I will continue to trust Him.

"Let us hold unswerving to the hope we profess, for He who promised is faithful." (Hebrews 10:23 NIV)

Will you choose to trust Him no matter what you're going through right now? Will you bring Satan low by holding fast to your confidence in the loving will of our Savior? Will you dare to hope in every situation, not because you are worthy but because "worthy is the Lamb who was slain?"

Progress Is Found in the Pursuit of Holiness

How do we know we're making progress in our spiritual lives? I am convinced that progress is found in the *pursuit of holiness*. No matter what we're dealing with, big or small, it's what is on the inside that matters most in our battles.

"What lies behind you and what lies in front of you, pales in comparison to what lies inside of you." (attributed to Ralph Waldo Emerson)

Here is how I now measure progress in my spiritual life: Am I growing in my heartfelt love for the Lord? Am I learning to trust the Lord more and more in my mind? Am I staying faithful to the Lord in my words and deeds? Am I growing in my faith alongside my friends and family?

That is progress, no matter what I'm going through on the outside. After all, we are powered from the *inside out* by the Holy Spirit. For this reason, I pray daily that the Holy Spirit will fill my heart, mind, and soul, giving me strength and the wisdom to always surrender, trust, and obey the Lord. I accept my responsibility to pursue holiness.

"Come near to God and He will come near to you." (James 4:8a NIV)

Progress doesn't come from prosperity, from accomplishments, or from anything else on this earth. It comes from drawing ever closer to God.

"Do not love the world or anything in the world. If anyone loves the world, love for the Father is not in them. For everything in the world—the lust of the flesh, the lust of the eyes, and the pride of life—comes not from the Father but from the world. The world and its desires pass away, but whoever does the will of God lives forever." (1 John 2:15-17 NIV)

We are only able to grow closer to the Lord, to increase in holiness, become stronger in faith, and love the Lord more with His help. We are not meant to pursue holiness alone. God gives us friends and family to encourage us. He gives us His Word to feed us. He gives us His Holy Spirit to empower us.

"The LORD your God is in your midst, a mighty one who will save; he will rejoice over you with gladness; he will quiet you by his love; he will exult over you with loud singing." (Zephaniah 3:17 ESV)

Whatever you're going through, the Lord wants to guide and comfort you. He wants to love and lead you. He wants to be your source of joy and peace. He wants to help you grow stronger in your faith in every way.

It's important to remember that our destination, as we pursue holiness, is not of this world. Real joy, real beauty, real peace, and real success are found in the Lord, and when we desire these things, we are drawn heavenward.

"The best and most beautiful things in the world cannot be seen or even touched—they must be felt with the heart." (Helen Keller)

In the midst of disappointments, pain, setbacks, and tragedy, you can still make progress in the pursuit of holiness every day because God is with you, and His love never fails. Seek Him. Pray daily that the Holy Spirit will help you surrender, trust, and obey.

"Love always protects, always trust, always hopes, always perseveres." (1 Corinthians 13:7 NIV)

In the pursuit of holiness, the true prize is heaven.

Jesus Is Calling. Just Say Yes!

Jesus calls us to have a daily relationship with Him. No matter what we're facing in life, He wants us to walk with Him, but we must *choose* to trust Him even when we're in the midst of our toughest battles.

"It is God who arms me with strength and makes my way perfect." (Psalm 18:32 NIV)

It is so hard sometimes to trust God when we don't have an answer to our *why*. We see so much sin and hate and hurt all around us. Life can be so unfair. We're all so weak and sinful. We just want to understand it, but the Lord asks us to trust Him anyway.

We can get consumed with asking *why*. We can get so caught up in wanting to know the *reason* for our hardships that we get stuck in a dark place. The blame, doubt, anger, and sadness take root, and soon we can't see the Lord clearly. Don't you know this is exactly what Satan wants?

"From the ends of the earth I call to you, I call as my heart grows faint; lead me to the rock that is higher than I." (Psalm 61:2 NIV)

Here's the thing: God has all the answers. We don't need to know the *whys*. He knows what lies behind us and ahead of us. He knows what is inside of us, and He understands His purpose in everything. We don't need to know the *whys!* We only need to trust Him.

"For we live by believing and not by seeing." (2 Corinthians 5:7 NLT)

Don't let the *whys* of your situation drag you into a dark place where you can no longer see Him. Put your past, present, and future in His hands, even if they don't make sense. Turn everything over to Him continuously in prayer.

"Do not be anxious about anything, but in every situation, by prayer and petition, with thanksgiving, present your requests to God. And the peace of God, which transcends all understanding, will guard your hearts and your minds in Christ Jesus." (Philippians 4:6-7 NIV)

The reason you don't need to know the *why* of every situation is because God has already made clear His *end goal* for your life: heaven. He is leading you there. On good days and bad, trust Him with the journey. Let go of the need to understand. Walk in freedom. Walk in His love and let Him lead you to eternal life.

I Am Blessed so I May Be
a Blessing

God is my guiding light, always showing me the way. He is the Rock on which I stand firm, no matter what I'm dealing with in my life. He is my strength when I am weak. In every situation, good or bad, God is love, reminding me continually that I matter. He hears my prayers, He knows me, and He enables me to have a victorious life.

I have experienced this countless times in the last twenty-nine months, at my best and at my worst, as I have walked through the valley. I must constantly remind myself of this because Satan wants me to sit around and feel sorry for myself, or worry about the future, or wonder why this happened to me.

"For Christ's sake, I delight in weaknesses, in insults, in hardships, in persecutions, in difficulties. For when I am weak, then I am strong." (2 Corinthians 12:10 NIV)

Yet, I have also learned that the Lord has not blessed me in all of these ways simply for my sake. On the contrary, God loves me so that I can love others. This begins with friends and family, the people who know me, who have seen my ugly side, yet still pray for me and support me. They make me want to be a better man. God has put them in my life so that we may mutually love, encourage, and build up each other in the faith. We share our lives together. We share laughter and tears, but most of all, we share our prayers.

Of course, this love from God, at work in us and through us, is meant to be shared far beyond our circle of friends. For every blessing He gives, He desires us to share that blessing with everyone around us. When we are blessed, we are to respond by becoming a blessing to others.

"Now this I say, he who sows sparingly will also reap sparingly, and he who sows bountifully will also reap bountifully." (2 Corinthians 9:6 NIV)

Has God given you wisdom through His Word? Share it with others. Has He met your needs? Help meet the needs of others. Has He strengthened you when you were weak? Strengthen others. Has He surrounded you with people to pray for you and encourage you? Pray for and encourage others.

We can get so caught up in our own battles that we forget God's purpose is to move *through us* into the lives of other people. Be a blessing to someone today!

"A generous person will prosper; whoever refreshes others will be refreshed." (Proverbs 11:25 NIV)

The Weight of the World

My battle with cancer can be all-consuming, even on my good days. It's easy to let the weight of this war bring me down, so I have to be diligent in my faith. This is another reason why I call it "Satan's Cancer."

The enemy wants me to doubt God's love for me. He wants me to feel unworthy, to focus on the pain, to worry about the future, or just to get so wrapped up in my own suffering that all I think about is *me*. Satan wants to keep piling on anxieties until I am crushed under the weight of them. To do this, he doesn't just use my own personal battles. He also wants to overwhelm me—to overwhelm each of us—with the weight of the world.

Satan wants us so wrapped up in all the world's evils that the weight of it becomes unbearable and makes faith almost impossible. "Look at all the wicked people in the world! Look at all the evil being done! Look at all the sin and sickness! Don't you realize it's hopeless?"

The fact is, we are not able to bear the weight of the world. It's too much. Our only hope is to entrust everything to the Lord, place everything in His hands, and trust Him *no matter what.*

"Many are the woes of the wicked, but the Lord's unfailing love surrounds the one who trusts in Him." (Psalm 32:10 NIV)

I can't carry the burdens on my own. You can't carry the burdens on your own. Beyond our own personal battles, the world is just *too much*. Put everything, absolutely everything, in the Lord's hands daily.

Every day, as soon as I get up, I pray and recommit myself to the Lord. I remind myself that He is always with me. I pray that He will help me to trust Him and listen to Him no matter what Satan throws at me, no matter what the world throws at me, because I know this is the only way I'm going to make it.

There is too much evil in the world for one mind, one heart, one soul to bear, so don't try! Instead, entrust yourself to the all-powerful love of God. Your responsibility is to love the Lord and follow Him. That's it. Everything else is up to Him.

"God's will is not an itinerary, but an attitude." (Andrew Dhuse)

"Be joyful in hope, patient in affliction, faithful in prayer. Share with the LORD'S people who are in need. Practice hospitality." (Romans 12:12-13 NIV)

Put *absolutely everything* in the Lord's hands. Don't try to carry the weight of the world. You can't do it! Let the Lord carry it all. He can, and He will!

The Power of Prayer

Often, when I am praying silently to the Lord, I feel Jesus asking me, "Do you love Me? Do you trust Me? Do you truly have faith in Me?"

"Yes, Lord, I love You," I reply. "Yes, I trust You. Yes, I have faith in You. You are the foundation of my life. Your love, wisdom, and power have brought me victory in this ongoing battle."

These times of prayer have become a regular part of my day, and I can feel them continually building my relationship with God. Through His comfort, through His presence, through His peace, He strengthens my faith and keeps me close.

Through prayer, combined with His Word, God guides my thoughts and directs my actions, helping me to become a better person.

"I used to believe that prayer changes things, but now I know that prayer changes us, and we change things." (Mother Teresa)

I don't pray to change God. I pray because I am changed. During those moments when I speak to Him, when I listen to Him, I feel His love, I receive His grace and mercy, and I am empowered to do good in the world.

We should be praying continually not to twist God's arm or bend His will, but to allow Him to change us for the better. This is the real power of prayer!

Sharing My Ugliness

I had scans done this week, and the results were very encouraging. It seems like the drugs are working and controlling the cancer. My PSA, which peaked at 1,400, is down to a new low of 0.46. Glory to God! What a gift! But, of course, God's real gift isn't the positive outcome of my ongoing battle with cancer. Even if my health took a turn for the worse, I would still possess God's truest and best gift: Jesus, who loves us and died for us. I am particularly mindful of this because another Christmas season is upon us as I write this.

"For God so loved the world that He gave His one and only Son, that whoever believes in Him shall not perish but have eternal life." (John 3:16 NIV)

"Then the Grinch thought of something he hadn't before. Maybe Christmas, he thought, doesn't come from a store. Maybe Christmas, perhaps, means a little bit more!" (Dr. Seuss, *How the Grinch Stole Christmas*)

Making the most of this gift means becoming utterly dependent on the love Jesus has for us. To do that, we have to slow down and listen more. We have to trust His wisdom for our lives. We have to allow His love for us to guide our actions, no matter what we're going through.

But I have to be honest with myself. I was born a sinner, and I am incapable of doing the right thing all the time. God already knows this. In fact, He knew everything there is to know about me before I was born. Therefore, I can share all of my ugliness with Him. I can take my hurt, my anxieties, and my failures and bring them to the Lord, wholly trusting them to His Love. There is no sense in holding back.

"You have searched me, Lord, and You know me. You know when I sit and when I rise; You perceive my thoughts from afar. You discern my going out and my lying down; You are familiar with all my ways." (Psalm 139:1-3 NIV)

God never asked us to pretend like we have it all together. He never expects us to act like we're perfect. He knows our weaknesses. He has always known. That is why Jesus took our sins to the cross, so that those who believe in Him, as imperfect as we are, might have the hope of eternal life.

Remember, Jesus is a Counselor. We can share everything with Him—the good, the bad, and the ugly—because He already knows every hair on our heads. He never asked us to "fake it until we make it." He wants us to bring all of that ugliness to Him and let His love deal with it. This is the power of God's greatest gift!

Blessed by Hardship

Another new year is upon me, and I think back to the beginning of my battle with cancer. After my diagnosis, a friend of mine told me that his cancer, which he learned about on his fortieth birthday, was the best present he'd ever received.

Since I had just been diagnosed with stage IV cancer when he told me this, I thought, "How in the world can he say that? Is he nuts?"

Now, more than two years down the road, I understand. Because of cancer, I learned what it truly means to be strong in the Lord when we are weak. Because of cancer, I became a better person. Because of cancer, I now know how to fight!

"With God we will gain the victory." (Psalm 60:12a NIV)

God taught me how to stop worrying constantly. He taught me how to trust Him even in sickness and weakness. He taught me to pray continually. I received all of these blessings as a result of the worst news of my life.

"Blessed is the one who perseveres under trial because, having stood the test, that person will receive the crown of life that the Lord has promised to those who love Him." (James 1:12 NIV)

Because of cancer, I am closer to God, closer to my friends and family, and more faithful in prayer. I am also learning how to let go of the past. Satan's old tactic of getting me bogged down with blame, guilt, or feeling sorry for myself, trying to make me feel depressed or unworthy—these tactics used to be very effective in my life.

Because of cancer, the Lord has taught me to *let go and move on.*

Satan would also like for me to get stuck in reliving the good old days. "Oh, things used to be great way back when. They'll never be that great again!" The Lord is teaching me to let go of this as well. The best days are always *yet to come.*

The Lord has given me more time than I thought I would have. That first year, when the doctor told me to put my things in order, I thought my time on the earth was over, but as a result of this battle, I've learned to take one day at a time. God taught me how to focus on doing good in the moment rather than worrying about how much more time I have.

Yes, through my worst experience, I am able to say, "I did not and I will not give up." I learned to fight for what is good. I learned that my plans may change. I learned to trust God. I learned that God is good all the time. I learned that it is less and less about me. I learned that it is always more and more about God's love. I learned to stay committed to good no matter how bad it may seem.

What a blessing!

"In his heart a man plans his course, but the LORD determines his steps." (Proverbs 16:9 NIV)

Will you dare to trust God with your worst experiences?

Are you willing to see all of the good things He has taught you as a result of those experiences?

Are you able to be thankful in every circumstance?

"According to your faith let it be done to you." (Matthew 9:29b NIV)

Swimming Upstream

Once again, I am so blessed by my pastor's sermons. On Sunday, Pastor Ronnie Floyd shared a message titled, "Life Against the Flow: How to Live Upstream in a Godless Culture." As always, there was so much to think about and so much wisdom to apply to my life.

It is important to find a good church that really pours into you. Cross Church has been a true blessing—such a great place of worship and fellowship for me. I always feel recharged afterward, ready for the week ahead. God doesn't intend for any of us to fight our battles alone. We need the resources of a faithful church.

This battle of mine has been a lot like swimming upstream. I rarely have a moment to rest. My doctor told me that, in the beginning, he didn't think I would need more than one of my six-month injections. The cancer was so bad he didn't think I would live long enough to need more than that. My fight for life was one day at a time.

I received my sixth injection in December. I thanked my doctor for being one of God's great resources. But I know I would not have had the strength to swim upstream this long if I had not been surrounded by a Godly community of prayerful people.

Today, my faith is as strong as it has ever been. I am surrounded by more prayer than I could ever have hoped for. But I look out at the world and see this culture and it's so hard not to get discouraged. I never thought I would live to see a day where we are so bitterly divided about what is right and wrong.

"If we in the church want a cause to fight, let's fight sin. Let's reveal its hideousness. Let's show that Jeremiah was correct when he said, 'The heart is deceitful above all things, and desperately wicked.'" (Billy Graham)

I can't just think about and pray about myself. I have to care about the world around me. What difference can I make in this nation, where Satan's schemes seem to be working? What can I do about the madness that has gripped this country?

I know I can't carry the weight of the world, as I've said before, but I can make a difference. It starts with me. I must choose to live a good life by entrusting myself fully to God. He will help me to swim upstream against the ugliness that seems to have filled the world.

"Moral living sometimes demands difficult choices. It requires selflessness." (Billy Graham)

When we are surrounded by evil, God wants us to shine, not succumb.

"Do everything without grumbling or arguing, so that you may become blameless and pure, children of God without fault in a warped and crooked generation. Then you will shine among them like stars in the sky as you hold firmly to the word of life." (Philippians 2:14-16a NIV)

Sometimes, the combination of our personal struggles and the ugliness we see in the world around us seems like too much, but God's mighty hand is with us. He will guide and protect us. We don't have to fear the ugliness of the world. We don't have to despair.

He provides the strength we need to keep swimming upstream and not wear out.

Focus on the Lord's will because His will wins in the end!

The Importance of Lunch

I had the opportunity to catch up with an old friend today over lunch at P.F. Chang's. What a great godly friend, and the time we shared was so encouraging. I don't know why we let so much time pass without seeing each other, but I am committed to making sure we meet up again soon.

Women are so much better at this than men. They understand the value of spending time with friends. Men, we have to figure this out! Too many men are isolated. They go into their man caves and never come out. We have to start making time to stay connected with friends and acquaintances, whether it's for lunch, coffee, or just a quick phone call, even a text!

We *need* this kind of fellowship. It is not wasted time. Time spent together is good for the heart, good for the mind, and good for the soul. Men, we need this just as much as women! It is not manly to keep to yourself. God designed you for fellowship.

I'm sure there are some women who need this encouragement as well. That godly friend that you haven't spoken to in a long time for no particular reason? Maybe it's time for a text, an email, a phone call, a card. Invite them to lunch or coffee. Get together! We need each other.

We are influenced by the people we surround ourselves with, so envelop yourself with positive people. Don't let a godly friend slip away.

Stay in touch and find reasons to get together. Let them build you up, and build them up in return. Just a friendly conversation now and again can work wonders.

"You know how you can find God's love? It's in God's people." (Titus Grigg)

At the end of our meal at P.F. Chang's, I got a fortune cookie. It said, "A simple kindness today will soon bring you unexpected rewards." Even though it's just a little writing on a piece of paper, I took it to heart. I hope it's true!

Of course, my fortune isn't found in a message pulled out of a cookie. Life is meant to be lived and shared, and my fortune is found by living and sharing God's love and wisdom with others. This is where God works most powerfully.

"But I do not want to be blessed except to be a blessing. For you have shown me that there is a greater blessedness than to be blessed without being a blessing. For this greater blessedness I plead – the blessedness to be a blessing." (John Piper)

The Necessity of Tough Love

It has now been thirty-three months since I was first diagnosed with stage IV prostate cancer. Since then, the battle has dominated my life. It's certainly not what I had planned for this phase of my life. Every day, I have to get up and continue the fight, even though I am weak and prone to sin.

"Christians aren't fighting *for* victory. Christians fight *from* a place of victory." (Dr. Robert Jeffress)

Every day, I remind myself that I will have victory in the end, no matter how rough the battle becomes, because I know God and His love wins. I get up every morning and thank Him for the time He gives me. After all, I was not expected to survive. I was told to get my things in order, but here I am thirty-three months later, still going strong.

"Prayer is for every moment of our lives, not just for times of suffering or joy. Prayer is really a place, a place where you meet God in genuine conversation." (Billy Graham)

Though I am stronger in my faith than ever, though I am surrounded by people who pray for me, still I have to fight against anxiety, worry, doubt, and fear. We all do. It helps to have friends and family with whom you can share all of these struggles, but you can share them with the Lord as well. He already knows.

"Don't you think God would rather have you be honest with Him about your doubts than have you profess a phony faith? He knows what's going on inside us anyway." (Lee Strobel)

Sometimes, I confess, I can be a bit phony with my friends. It's not always easy to be honest about our struggles, is it? When people ask us how we're doing, we're tempted to say, "I'm fine. No problem. I feel good."

My friends don't let me get away with those kinds of answers. They see right through me, and they dig deeper. They know when I need a little *tough love* to help me be honest about my struggles.

It's important to let your friends push back. Give them permission to be a little tough on you. We all need people in our lives who challenge us to be honest, who help us push through whatever is holding us back, who keep us moving forward and making progress. Your friends aren't doing that if they feel like they have to tiptoe around you.

Give your loved ones permission to show tough love. It prevents us from feeling sorry for ourselves. It makes us get up and keep going, even when we don't think we can. It helps us put things back in the proper perspective.

Whether we're on the mountaintop or in the deepest valley, we all need a little tough love to keep us moving in the right direction. My friends and family are free to call me out on my foolishness, or ask me difficult questions, or confront me about their concerns. They can tell me when I'm wrong. I receive it from them because I know it's good for me.

No matter how tough they might be from time to time, I know they care about me, and they have my best interests in mind. A little tough love is okay. Be open to it. Let those who care about you challenge you to keep pushing forward. Be willing to sometimes show the same toughness to them, as long as it always comes from love.

"Let us consider how we may spur one another on toward love and good deeds." (Hebrews 10:24 NIV)

Keeping My Fear in the
Right Place

It has now been three years since my life, and the lives of those around me, changed forever. Three years ago, I went for a physical and encountered the *fear of all fears.*

From that point on, I learned the importance of managing fear. We all have things we worry about, but in that moment, I was overwhelmed: Am I going to die? What will happen to my family? Am I going to experience pain? Why did this happen to me? Did I do something wrong?

In a time of trouble, fear can absolutely take over your life if you let it. I saw how easily this could happen, so I went to my knees. I immediately started praying, and I asked all of my loved ones to pray with me. I did this not just because I wanted God's help in the fight against cancer, but also because I wanted to *replace the fear* with hope.

You see, it's not just the trouble that can defeat you. It's the fear the trouble produces. Fear can consume everything good in your life. In the aftermath of my diagnosis, I first had to accept that I had cancer. I had to come to terms with it so it wouldn't control my life. Then I had to put my future in God's hands, letting go of my plans completely. In doing so, I realized that the fight wasn't really about cancer—it was about entrusting myself fully to God with my past, present, and future.

A big part of fear, after all, is about losing control, relinquishing our plans, trying to hold on to things rather than handing them over to the Lord. God wants us to learn to depend entirely on His love and the resources He provides us every day. This is what brings true peace, cutting through every fear and helping us walk in freedom.

With every twist and turn in my battle, I feel fear trying to gain a foothold, so surrendering myself to the Lord has to be a daily choice. By the grace of God, He gives me peace in every circumstance when I continually put everything in His hands. I know I am surrounded by Jesus and His love. He will protect my heart and my mind, as long as I turn to Him, right up to the very end of my life.

Three years ago, I was filled with fear. Today, as a result of the battle, I know how to take my fears and turn them over to God in prayer. What a tremendous blessing this has been! The Lord is the One who keeps our fears in check! Turn everything over to Him today. Trust Him fully with your past, present, and future, and let Him lead you to where He wants you to go.

"So do not fear, for I am with you; do not be dismayed, for I am your God. My righteous right hand." (Isaiah 41:10 NIV)

Maintaining the Bricks

Slow down. Speed up. Do this. Do that. Do both! Stop! Don't do that! Okay, what's next?

That's how my life has felt these past three years. There is always something that needs to be done. I seem to be constantly busy with work, treatment, family responsibilities, etc. But I am thankful for every day, even with my full to-do list.

Nevertheless, I have to be careful in the *doing* that I never forget the importance of *being*. My purpose is less about what I *do* and more about *who I am* in the Lord.

"Nothing can calm our souls more or better prepare us for life's challenges than time spent alone with God." (Billy Graham)

With age and experience, I have learned the importance of keeping the foundation of my life strong. Every brick needs to be maintained: through prayer, through God's Love, through the wisdom of His Word, through fellowship. I can't let the busyness of my life cause me to neglect the foundation of who I am.

You don't want to get so caught up in all the things you have to do that you fail to notice the foundation of your life cracking and crumbling beneath you. Before you know it, all sorts of sin and strife will start to slip through the cracks.

"Take care of the tiniest detail because the little details add up until they represent significant differences. Let nothing slip through the cracks." (Bill Belichick)

Instead of worrying about everything you have to do in the future, just concentrate on the very next step, so you can put most of your focus on maintaining the foundation of your life, brick by brick: pray continually, share God's love and His Word, stay in fellowship, grow in holiness, and keep drawing near to God.

Every day, I pray for the Holy Spirit to teach me and guide me, so that each brick God has placed in the foundation of my life remains firmly in place, strong and unyielding to the enemy's schemes.

"So, I say, walk by the Spirit, and you will not gratify the desires of the sinful nature." (Galatians 5:16 NIV)

Don't Fret the Whys

Even now, after all I've been through, I still struggle with the *whys*.

"Why the hurt? Why the loss? Why the pain? Why me? Why cancer?"

These kinds of questions lead nowhere. They just create doubt, anxiety, confusion, envy, and fear. They fill my mind with endless thoughts that prevent me from focusing on what matters most. This is exactly what Satan wants, to get my mind off my faith, family, friends, and *fighting the good fight*.

"Focus on Christ instead of your fears, and your fears will begin to fade." (Billy Graham)

When my kids were little, they always used to ask me why, especially about things they didn't like. "Why do I have to clean my room? Why do we have to go to school? Why do we have to eat vegetables?" Finally, after the tenth time, I would say something like, "You just do. Trust me. I'm your father." I feel like that is exactly the answer the Lord has given me after I've asked him a thousand times, "Why did this happen to me?"

"I am your Father, and my love is always with you. Trust me, trust my wisdom, and have faith. I have a purpose in all of this!"

There are so many things in life that we will never understand this side of heaven. In all of them, we must simply trust God and His wisdom.

If He didn't have a purpose—a good purpose—for it, it wouldn't have happened. Continue to walk by faith, stay in fellowship, and go to Him continually in prayer.

"The Lord is my light and my salvation—whom shall I fear? The Lord is the stronghold of my life—of whom shall I be afraid?" (Psalm 27:1 NIV)

It all comes down to a simple choice: are we going to trust God with our lives or not? God shares His wisdom with us, but even when we don't fully understand, will we still choose to trust Him fully with our lives?

"God's plan for your life is greater than your plan. Plan less and trust more." (Jon Gordon)

"Above all, don't be satisfied with anything less than God's will for your life." (Billy Graham)

It Is Not a Coincidence

God knows what He's doing, and He has a purpose in everything. God created everything, seen and unseen. He is Father, Son, and Holy Spirit—three in One.

"For from Him and through Him and for Him are all things. To Him be the glory forever! Amen." (Romans 11:36 NIV)

My faith is in the Great Almighty, the all-knowing and all-powerful God, Who was and is and is to come. When God is with us, who can be against us? It's important to remind ourselves of *who God is* when life seems unfair, when we seem to be slipping, or when we've done wrong. We can always go to God humbly in prayer with any problem. There is no reason to wait.

Nothing that we go through in life is a coincidence. God has a purpose for everything we experience: for every struggle, for every hardship, for every blessing. In our brokenness, our weakness, and our pain, He wants to teach us about His Love, so that we can rejoice that there is always hope.

"Be joyful in hope, patient in affliction, faithful in prayer." (Romans 12:12 NIV)

Hope is not a coincidence either. It happens when we are patient, constant in prayer, and steadfast in our faith in God's love. It is no coincidence that I became stronger in my battle against Satan's cancer, because cancer made me desperate for God's love and grace. In that desperation, I chose to pray every day—many times a day. I pray so much now that I truly know what it is like to be "living on a prayer."

It is no coincidence that God placed my friends and family around me, because we have helped each other to become stronger in faith as we fight our battles together. By sharing the ups and downs in this crazy thing we call *life*, we have become resources of God in each other's lives. There are no coincidences! God places people into our lives for a reason, and sometimes He removes people from our lives for a reason. In either case, we must trust the Lord's purpose, whether we see it or not.

"Sometimes God removes a person from your life for your own protection. Do not run after them. Trust God. He knows what He's doing." (Rick Warren)

We all have our own battles, but we must never forget that we are all fighting the good fight together as we move ever closer to heaven. Someday, all of His purposes in every situation will be revealed. Until then, pray for strength, wisdom, and courage.

Darkness Can Be the Beginning, Not the End

As a child, I was afraid of the dark. I hated my closet, and I always worried about what was underneath my bed. Darkness can be a scary place. Fortunately, I know that darkness can never overcome the light of Christ. Often, His light shines brightest when we're in a very dark place.

"I have come into the world as a light, so that no one who believes in Me should stay in darkness." (John 12:46 NIV)

When I find myself in a dark place, I have to remember that I'm not alone. In Christ, we are never alone. His light is always with us, so we can confront our fears. Just as I have outgrown my childhood fear of the dark, I have grown in my faith to understand that sometimes our darkest times in life are a new beginning for our faith and our confidence in Christ's love.

I know now that I can't always avoid the darkness. It finds a way to sneak into my life, and those times are full of hurt, confusion, anxiety, anger, denial, and a lot of "why me." It gets messy in the darkness. We find ourselves stumbling over the clutter of our lives.

"Out of clutter, find simplicity. From discord, find harmony. In the middle of difficulty lies opportunity." (Albert Einstein)

However, in the darkness, in the clutter, in our stumbling and our pain, we have the perfect opportunity to turn on the light of Christ and shine His brightness into every corner. With His Light shining brightly through us, we can see the clutter, which keeps us from stumbling. We can see the good that God has placed before us.

With His light shining in the darkest places, we always have hope.

"Hope begins in the dark, the stubborn hope that if you just show up and try to do the right thing, the dawn will come. You wait and watch and work: You don't give up." (Anne Lamott)

How do we shine with the light of Christ in our darkest places?

By continuing to trust Him, no matter what.

By crying out in prayer continuously.

By committing ourselves to do His will.

This is sometimes easier said than done, so we can only take it one day at a time. Fortunately, His light, which shines down on us from heaven, shows us the right path, so we know where to place our next footstep.

"Do everything without grumbling and arguing, so, that you may be blameless and pure, children of God who are faultless in a crooked and perverted generation, among whom you shine like stars in the world." (Philippians 2:14-15)

The light of Christ can never shine too brightly. Don't hold back. Let it shine so brightly in you and through you that His love and light reflect on everything around you.

I look at my fight with cancer, at the darkness of those days, as the beginning of a better and stronger me. I shine more brightly now because the darkness made me aware of my need and drove me to Him.

Let His light shine—all the time!

Greater Is the Spirit
Within Me

This week I went in for more scans to see what's going on with the cancer in my body. I prayed that the cancer was still asleep, and I trusted the Holy Spirit, knowing that He that is within me is always greater!

"The One who is in you is greater than the one who is in the world." (1 John 4:4b NIV)

Because of the Holy Spirit within me, I am confident and ready for any trials I might face. Thankfully, the scans showed that the cancer has not changed since I got the last scans a year ago. All glory be to God!

I didn't ask for this cancer. It wasn't a choice I made for my life, but I also didn't choose to be born in sin. I am weak, I am broken, and I am always in need of God's love and forgiveness.

"You are more broken than you think and more loved than you can comprehend." (Cody Hollister)

Even though I admit to my own brokenness, I try not to dwell on it. I can't dwell on mistakes I've made. The past is the past. Only one perfect soul has ever walked this earth: our Lord and Savior Jesus Christ, a gift from our Father in heaven.

So, I know I am not alone in my weakness, my brokenness, my sin. Still, I must accept that the Lord has a better way for me.

"Jesus said to him, 'I am the way, the truth, and the life. No one comes to the Father except through Me." (John 14:6 NIV)

God's better way works from the inside out. I pray daily that the Holy Spirit will fill my heart, mind, and soul, enabling me to surrender fully to His way, to trust His truth, and to always know that He is leading me home to my Father in heaven. Through hardship, through weakness and brokenness, through forgiveness, through it all, He is leading me home.

The Holy Spirit within me is greater than my cancer, greater than any sickness, any trial, any temptation, any schemes of the devil or anything this world puts in my path. I know He intends for me to learn from my hardships, but He also intends for me to learn from my sins and mistakes. We are loved more than we can ever comprehend, but in our brokenness, He is always showing us the right way to go.

"I put my identity in what Christ says, who He thinks I am, and who I know that He says I am." (Trevor Lawrence)

We fight the good fight from the inside out, above all, by trusting God and His work in us and through us. Looking at the world around me today, I've never seen a greater need for people to get back to the old motto, "In God We Trust."

We all need the Spirit working within us to make us wiser, stronger, and more faithful. Only by a transformation on the inside can we successfully fight our battles on the outside. That's the key!

The war within is the *real war*.

No matter what you're facing, no matter the wrongs you have done, no matter the battle you are in, He who is within you is greater than *anything.* Win the war within. Entrust yourself fully to the Holy Spirit every day, and make the choice to trust God in every situation.

Let's commit to fighting the good fight together!

The Best Is Yet to Come

In the battle between my faith and Satan's cancer, I have come to understand that I will never be perfect. There are a million ways for me to become a better man, and the best is always yet to come.

Of course, it's easy to say the best is yet to come when you're in the deepest valley, when you've fallen all the way to the bottom and there's nowhere to look but up. Can I still say it when I'm on the mountaintop? When I have a great day, when I'm overflowing with tremendous blessings, can I still strive to grow and become a better man? Can I still say, "The best is yet to come?"

Because it's true. No matter where you are in life, or what kind of day you're having, no matter what you're going through, whether you're in the deepest valley, on the mountaintop, or somewhere in between—in Christ, the best is always yet to come.

What a privilege it is to know this.

priv·i·lege /*priv(ə)lij*/ "a special right, advantage, or immunity granted or available only to a particular person or group."

What a privilege it is to be part of God's family, surrounded by brothers and sisters in Christ, fighting the good fight of faith with the Father of all fathers, the King of all kings, the great, almighty Creator of heaven and earth, of all that is seen and unseen.

For all who have accepted Jesus into their hearts, surrendered to His ways, trusted in His love, and are fighting the good fight of faith every day, two things remain: to know absolutely that you are never alone and to realize that the best is yet to come.

I can only imagine the great day when I finally see heaven. Nothing in this world could possibly compare.

"We all die. The goal isn't to live forever, the goal is to create something that will." (Chuck Palahniuk)

You can have this world; give me Jesus. What a privilege it will be when I am finally called home to be with Him. Until then, I am blessed to be part of the Father's family, following Jesus, knowing that He alone is "the way, the truth, and the life" (John 14:6).

This same privilege is freely available to all who accept Jesus into their hearts, surrender, and trust His love and His Word.

"Through the written Word, we discover the Living Word, Jesus Christ." (Billy Graham)

"Those who belong to Christ Jesus have crucified the flesh with its passions and desires. Since we live by The Spirit, let us keep in step with the Spirit. Let us not become conceited, provoking and envying each other." (Galatians 5:24-25 NIV)

Many of the earthly privileges that we perceive to be honorable are nothing more than schemes of Satan to create division, make us conceited, or tempt us to envy others. The "haves and have nots" does not apply to God's family, because He will accept anyone. He knows us from the inside out, and He brings us together, making us stronger in His love. No one needs to be left behind.

No matter how unworthy we might feel, no matter how broken we are, He loves us.

"If we are faithless, He remains faithful; He cannot deny Himself." (2 Timothy 2:13 NLT)

It is a privilege that I can pray and ask the Holy Spirit to fill my heart, mind, and soul every day. He gives me the strength and wisdom I need to surrender, trust, and obey God with every step I take, every word I speak, and every thought I have. The Holy Spirit gives me patience—not just the ability to wait, but control over how I act while I'm waiting. The Holy Spirit also gives me the joy I need to persist in this battle of mine and in this life of mine.

Every day I must strive to be better. I can't afford to worry about tomorrow when I'm getting ready for today, so I remind myself, "Today is the day I get better, stronger, and wiser."

"Therefore, do not worry about tomorrow, for tomorrow will worry about itself. Each day has enough trouble of its own." (Matthew 6:34 NIV)

With so many ways to improve myself, it could get overwhelming, so I try to keep it simple. To do that, I focus on four simple steps:

Step One: Accept and believe in the love of Jesus, sharing that love with others.

Step Two: Keep my faith in Jesus, surrendering, trusting, and obeying Him.

Step Three: Walk in repentance toward God, turning all of my sins, struggles, and brokenness over to Him.

Step Four: Repeat steps one through four.

In a way, step four is the most important, because there is always more to do, more to learn, more ways to grow. After all, the best is yet to come.

Repeat, repeat, repeat!

The best is yet to come, because heaven is the best there is!

Do you believe it?

Conclusion: What Comes Next?

I will never be cancer free. That's just a fact. The cancer has already spread throughout my body, but the treatments are working. My doctor does blood work every three months, and if all is well, I only have to do a full body scan once a year. I also receive an injection every six months and take a pill once a day to keep it in remission. That takes care of the physical battle, but it's faith, family, and friends—along with the power of prayer—that take care of the spiritual battle.

Journaling my battle has helped me to get my thoughts and feelings in order. It continues to provide me with a time of reflection, and it gives me peace in the midst of whatever I'm going through. As I like to say, a mind at peace brings healing to a body in need.

We're all broken in some way, aren't we? We were all born in sin and brokenness. Cancer serves as a reminder of this for me every day.

Journaling has helped me become more intentional about listening and learning. During sermons at church, I listen more intently than I used to. I'm more focused on the message, and I take notes. When I read a devotional book or Scripture, I reflect on the words and take notes.

I understand that God has a plan for me, and I've learned how to stay focused as I fight the good fight. Through cancer, doubt, pain, and fear,

I have a clearer sense of what is really important. I've come to understand that this battle is less about me and more about taking care of other people. If I can bring any hope to people who feel overwhelmed, who see only darkness and despair in their future, then all of my pain will have been worth it.

I no longer fear death. The battle has driven that fear out of me, and I believe more than ever that our true prize is not on Earth. We are being called heavenward! When my time comes to leave this life, I just want to finish strong, to hear the Lord say, "Well done, my good and faithful servant" (Matthew 25:21 NLT).

As for this book, the journey doesn't end here. We all need a community of people praying for us and encouraging us. I strongly encourage you to find a good church of loving people and get plugged in. Find a prayer group or Bible study. Open yourself up to a community. Encourage them as they encourage you. Spend time with friends and family. Don't try to fight your battle alone.

It's not always easy to open up and share your battles, but in sharing these journal entries with friends and family, my relationships became stronger. My family is stronger, more tight-knit, and abounding in faith more than ever before.

God walks side by side with us even in our deepest valleys. Put your trust in Him today; He will carry you Home.

I have set up a website where you can share your story, encourage and be encouraged, and continue to receive strength and hope for your journey. Please join us there at **TheDeepestValley.com**.

"So do not fear, for I am with you; do not be dismayed, for I am your God. I will strengthen you and help you; I will uphold you with My righteous right hand." (Isaiah 41:10 NIV)

"You are a warrior. Don't abandon your post or get distracted in the fight. You have someone to protect, a Kingdom to advance, and a battle to win!" (Craig Groeschel)

"Show me your friends, and I will show you your future." (Anonymous)

"Every change starts with one simple step." (Senior Pastor Nick Floyd, Cross Church)

Afterword

No matter how deep the valley, there is always hope to be found in faith, family, and friends. The best way to climb out of that valley is to put God first, others second, and yourself third.

Never forget, no matter the battle, our real calling is to fight the good fight of faith every day. That is the *real* fight, so keep it at the forefront of your mind and heart. It is greatest *prize fight* of all time, so let's face it together.

To my brothers and sisters in the faith, I thank you!

Dan Kallesen

To continue the journey, please join us at
TheDeepestValley.com

Printed in the USA
CPSIA information can be obtained
at www.ICGtesting.com
LVHW021414170923
758448LV00011B/505